Atlantic Ocean

Anguilla

St. John

Anegada

St. Martin

Puerto Rico

Tortola

Saba

Barbuda

San Juan *

St. Christopher

Antigua

St. Thomas

Nevis

Vieques

Montserrat

Marie
Galante

Guadeloupe

St. Croix

Dominica

N

Martinique

St. Lucia

Barbados

St. Vincent

Sea

W

E

Grenadines

Grenada

S

Bonaire

Margarita

Tobago

Curaçao

Trinidad

Aruba

Venezuela

The CARIBBEAN ISLANDS

HANS W. HANNAU

The Caribbean Islands

WITH **104** COLOR PHOTOGRAPHS AND **30** MAPS

ARGOS INC.
MIAMI

Cover Design (jacket) by Don Platt
End paper by Felix Kraus
Maps by Hedy Eibuschutz and Felix Kraus

ISBN: 0-89530-004-4
Composed in U.S.A., printed in Spain

Dep. Legal B-29,587-XV

INTRODUCTION

Had there not been a scent of land in the air, the mutinous Spanish sailors on the Pinta, the Niña and the Santa Maria might have forced Columbus to turn back to Spain and to sail into obscurity. But they smelled a special fragrance, saw lovely land birds flying above them, and picked up a fascinating land plant floating on the ocean. They sailed west, to glory.

They landed first on several islands in the Bahamas, and sailed from them to the Caribbean and north coast of Cuba. Columbus described the fertile, temperate and beautiful islands as the "best in the world." The foliage was green, the melody of the birds exquisite and the fragrance of the flowers "the sweetest thing in the world." Since Columbus stepped ashore in the West Indies men and women of many races have found the same special magic in those islands that so enchanted their first European discoverer.

The people who live in and love the Caribbean world today speak Spanish, English, French, Dutch and Portuguese. The dialects compounded from these languages are numerous. The skins of the people who talk these languages range in color from deepest black to albino white. On most of the islands there is equality and harmony among races.

Each of the islands has its own history, culture and tradition. The birds, the plants and the weather also differ among the islands. Some islands lie out of the swing of the seas that are bulldozed high by hurricane winds; some are storm-prone. Some are lush green; a few are arid.

With all their differences, though, the islands are in many ways one world. Geologically, they belong to what was once one land, much of which is now beneath the sea. Many of the high green hills are of ancient volcanic origin. The climate is frost-free, the trade winds silken and caressing. The waters that lap the beaches are always warm, pellucid and beautiful—green in the shallows and Gulf Stream blue in the great depths. But all the islands appeal to the senses. They make people who live there and those who visit happy to be alive, to sense and know the luscious fruits of the land and the sea.

The Spaniards were the first settlers from Europe, but today England has more connections with the islands than any other European nation. The United States, through purchases and treaties, is the second big nation with Caribbean ties. The United States acquired Puerto Rico by treaty after the Spanish-American war, and bought some fifty Virgin islands from Denmark. France is the third most important "outsider," with sovereignty over Martinique, Guadeloupe and other smaller islands. The federated islands of the Netherlands Antilles—Aruba, Bonaire, Curaçao, Saint Maarten, Saba and St. Eustatius—are co-partners with the Kingdom of the Netherlands and have certain autonomous powers within the federation. Haiti, Cuba and the Dominican Republic are independent, free of all European ties.

Today this world throbs with hope. Some of the islands, like Puerto Rico, Aruba and Curaçao, are prosperous and have a high standard of living. Other islands are just coming out of the dark ages, and are experiencing that splendid lift of spirit that comes when people, whose ancestors were enslaved, acquire power and responsibility. Change is in the air, and everywhere the winds say that it is change for the better.

Many of the islands have learned that tourism can be the base for a sound economy. They have seen that tourism can produce jobs for a great many people, a stable economy, healthy growth and attractive home towns for permanent residents. Benefits are reciprocal. Visitors find tropical sun, sand and seas; islands with fascinating histories and the flavor of foreign lands. Accommodations for tourists range from luxurious Mediterranean style hotels to quaint beach cottages.

The Caribbean islands are among the world's meccas in the accelerating modern trek toward the sun. Today's visitors find the golden sunshine as valuable as the yellow metal the Spaniards sought. And the vein of sunshine will not run out.

HISTORY

IN THE BEGINNING

The Indians who met Columbus when he landed in the Caribbean were, according to his account, "as naked as when born of their mothers, most handsome men and women." They were so white that if they protected themselves from the sun and air, "they would be as white as in Spain." They were Arawak Indians who traded their tame parrots for hawk bells and glass beads. They swam expertly and paddled log canoes across the water. They wove cotton cloth, and from it made hammocks *(hamaca)* which were quickly adopted by the European sailors. Their houses were palmetto thatched shelters and their main foods were a soft corn and fish. The Arawáks had come to the Caribbean islands and the Bahamas from northern South America. Gentle and tractable people, they were to be captured, enslaved and all but exterminated by the Spaniards.

Another people had also preceded the Spaniards to the Antilles. They were the fierce and warlike Caribs. "Carib" means "cannibal" in the Arawak language. Columbus encountered this pugnacious race on his second voyage to the island he called Guadeloupe. In one of their camps he found the remains of a young man being boiled, together with the meat of some parrots and geese. The ferocious Caribs discouraged the Spaniards from settling on the islands they occupied. There are a few Carib Indians still living in Dominica and St. Vincent today.

COLUMBUS SAILS WEST

In 1492 when Columbus took possession of the New World in the name of the King and Queen of Spain, he thought he was claiming the land that produced the spices, silk, gems and gold of the Indies. He expected to meet representatives of the Great Khan of Cathay, for it was to find China that he had sailed west. Instead, he met naked Lucayans, members of the Arawak tribe, gentle and primitive folk whom he called Indians. Some of them had small gold ornaments hanging from holes in their noses.

Columbus called the island on which he landed San Salvador. It is one of the easternmost islands of the Bahamas. The Lucayans indicated that the gold they wore had been found to the south. Columbus sailed in that direction, taking six Lucayans aboard ship so that they might learn Spanish and serve as interpreters. The Spaniards explored the Bahama islands now known as Rum Cay, Long Island, Crooked Island and the tiny cays of the Bahama Bank. The Indians he met told him of two larger islands which they called "Colba" (Cuba) and "Bofio" (Haiti).

On October 28, 1492, Columbus reached the north coast of Cuba. This land he named Juana, in honor of the son of King Ferdinand and Queen Isabella. In this beautiful country the Spaniards found more Indians. Though they searched for evidence of the Oriental civilization of the Great Khan, they found only native villages, with carved wooden statues, domestic dogs and cloth woven from a splendid long-staple cotton. A group of the explorers who made an expedition into the interior of Cuba found natives smoking a grass rolled into tubes which they called "tobacos."

From Cuba the expedition sailed to the north coast of Haiti and anchored in a harbor Columbus named Mole-St. Nicholas. St. Nicholas was a pope who had forbidden conversion by force and reproved cruelty to pagans. The harbor has the same name today. This island Columbus also claimed for Spain and named La Isla Española. Today it is called Hispaniola and includes both Haiti and the Dominican Republic.

In Haiti the explorers met a king, called "cacique" by the Indians. Columbus and the king dined together and traded Indian gold for Spanish bedspreads, amber beads and orange-flower water. On Christmas day of 1492 the Santa Maria went aground on the island of Hispaniola. Columbus and his men built a fort on the island. Today the coast of Hispaniola is much the same as when Columbus first described it. There are no more Arawaks, however. Black descendants of Africans are the natives who live along the beaches.

Columbus returned to Spain aboard the Niña, accompanied by the Pinta. The glowing accounts he gave of the islands resulted in seventeen ships setting forth with him on his second voyage to colonize the New World. He had recognized the pattern of the westerly trade winds and made the Atlantic crossing in twenty-one days. When he arrived at the settlement of Navidad on the northern coast of Hispaniola, he found it destroyed. He es-

tablished a second colony, Isabela, on the same shore. From Isabela he went on to the south coast of Cuba, and then to Jamaica, still searching for Marco Polo's Cathay.

The Spanish colonists succeeded in provoking the Indians to war, and in 1496 Columbus' brother Bartholomé led the Spaniards to the south coast of Hispaniola. There he founded Santo Domingo, the city that was to be the capital of the Spanish Indies for the next fifty years.

Columbus' third voyage in 1498 did not end happily. With a few volunteers Columbus discovered and explored Trinidad and made his first landfall on the continent of South America. But when he reached Santo Domingo, he found mutiny in progress. Two ships were sent back to Spain to report the rebellion. In the meanwhile malcontents had reported Columbus was a tyrant and Francisco de Bodadilla was sent from Spain to investigate. Although Columbus had succeeded in stopping the rebellion, in October, 1500, he was sent with his brother back to Spain under arrest.

Columbus was eventually exonerated by the King and Queen, and outfitted for a fourth voyage in 1502. His landfall in the Caribbean was Martinique. He rode out a hurricane off Hispaniola, anchored off Honduras and explored the coasts of Nicaragua, Costa Rica and Panama. He returned to Spain in 1504. His twelve years in the Caribbean had made him a rich man. He died in 1506. He had wished to be buried in Hispaniola, and in 1536 his body was removed from Spain and buried in the Cathedral at Santo Domingo.

COLUMBUS' FOUR VOYAGES

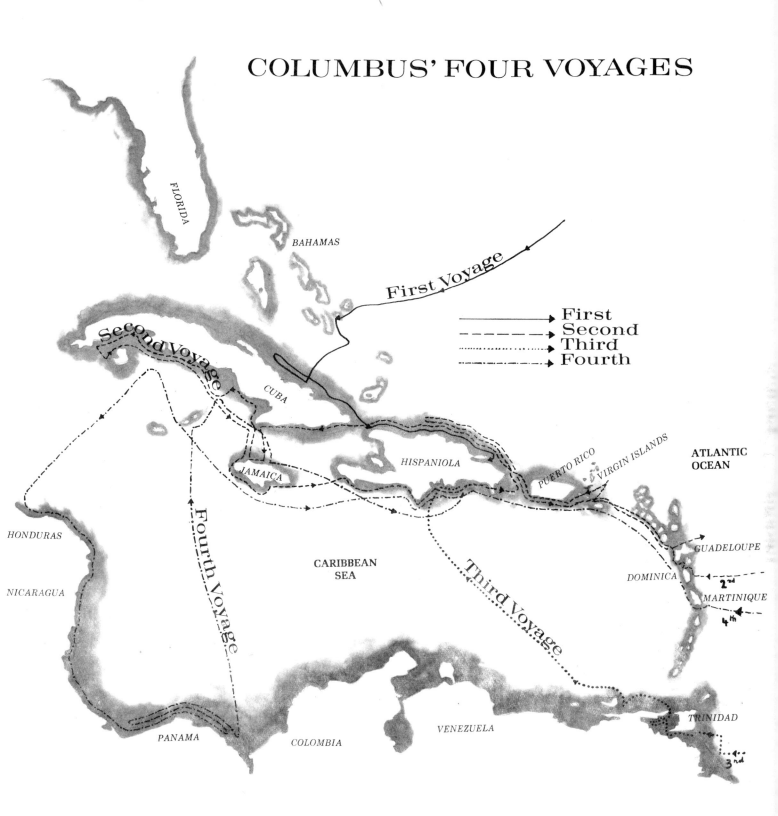

First Voyage

Second Voyage

Fourth Voyage

Third Voyage

First
Second
Third
Fourth

FLORIDA

BAHAMAS

CUBA

HISPANIOLA

PUERTO RICO

VIRGIN ISLANDS

ATLANTIC
OCEAN

JAMAICA

HONDURAS

NICARAGUA

CARIBBEAN
SEA

GUADELOUPE

DOMINICA

2nd

MARTINIQUE

4th

PANAMA

COLOMBIA

VENEZUELA

TRINIDAD

3rd

THE ERA OF SPANISH RULE

Santo Domingo remained the most important settlement in the Spanish Caribbean, and it grew rapidly. Gold was mined for two decades, though no great vein of treasure was found. Oranges, figs, lemons and bananas were introduced. Pigs and herds of wild cattle thrived, and hides and tallow were exported to Spain. Sugar, which was to shape the fate of the Caribbean for centuries, was introduced and the first sugar mill was built in Hispaniola in 1508. Sugar requires much unskilled labor for its cutting, and it must be milled as soon as it is cut. This led to attempts to enslave the Indians of the Caribbean and the Bahamas, but they fought or committed suicide. Blacks were brought from West Africa as slaves.

Jamaica was first settled by the Spanish in 1509, but Spain never considered the island important. It yielded no gold and was given over largely to cattle ranches in Spanish times.

Settlement of Cuba began in 1511 under the leadership of the energetic Diego Velazquez, a strict disciplinarian who launched the project as a private investment. Within three years his small force controlled the island, and in the first five years as governor he founded seven towns. The first was Santiago, the chief settlement until ships heading home to Spain by way of Florida channel north of Cuba brought Havana to the forefront.

With Balboa's discovery of the Isthmus of Panama and the Pacific coast in 1513, and Cortes' conquest of Mexico in 1519, the Caribbean islands became the highroad to the rich empire of which Spain had dreamed. For the first decades after Columbus' discovery, other European nations had paid little attention to Spain's colonies. When the Spainish ships began returning home laden with gold and silver, however, bold spirits from France, Holland and England began to descend upon the shipping. Spain attempted to control the import of good from Europe to the Caribbean, but smugglers of slaves and other necessities thrived by underselling the Spaniards.

Cattle-raising was originally the predominant source of income for the Spanish settlers, but sugar eventually became the major export. The demand was high in Europe for sugar, and as the investments in mills and slaves from West Africa increased, the exports increased.

THE CHALLENGES TO SPAIN

The English made their first settlement in the Caribbean in 1623 at St. Kitts in the Leeward Islands. Dutch traders took over several small islands—Aruba, Bonaire, Curaçao, Saba, St. Maarten and St. Eustatius—between 1630 and 1640: Today these islands are the Netherlands Antilles. The Dutch wanted them as bases for trade and fighting. When they were not fighting, they brought slaves out to the islands and took sugar and tobacco back home.

The French, not to be outdone, arrived not long after the English settled St. Kitts and also established a colony on that island. Martinique and Guadeloupe became French colonies in 1635. Saint-Domingue on Hispaniola was also settled by the French.

The English claimed Barbados (1624 or 1625) and in 1632 settled in Antigua and Montserrat. The English and Dutch jointly tried to settle the Virgin Islands at St. Croix about 1625. Britain went to war with Spain over Jamaica and took the island from the Spaniards in 1655. It is curious to note that in the 1640s the British white population in the West Indies peaked and since then has declined.

Competition for trade with the West Indies spurred on wars in Europe. England went to war against Spain and France many times between 1739 and 1763. Sugar from the colonies sparked the war between England and France in 1744. The attacks of each side on the other's colonies was simply an effort to put the competitor out of the business of producing sugar.

English and French rivalry flared into the Seven Years War in 1756. Spain came into that war in 1762, and an English fleet took Havana in the West Indies and Manila in the Pacific. England emerged victorious, but had to return some of the colonies that had been taken in order to get France and Spain to agree to a peace treaty. Many Englishmen argued that England should keep Guadeloupe in preference to Canada. However, in the end England received the whole continent of North America east of the Mississippi as settlement, including Canada and Florida. Martinique and Guadeloupe were returned to France and Cuba to Spain.

With the Peace of Paris, a great age dawned for the French West Indies. For three decades, until the French Revolution, the French colonies took the lead over the English in exporting sugar. The French sold their sugar, molasses and rum cheaper than the English, and this encouraged a brisk trade with the British colonies in North America. New England traders sold grain, salt fish, timber and horses to the French. Jamaica, Barbados and the British Leeward islands had passed their peak of sugar prosperity. Free ports had been established by the Dutch at St. Eustatius and Curaçao. After the war, the French developed a free port system on Martinique, Guadeloupe, St. Lucia and Saint-Domingue.

The American Revolution brought war and heavy taxes to the English islands. The English colonists in the British West Indies remained loyal to England. France got into the fighting in 1778 and Spain in 1779. The French captured Dominica, St. Vincent and Grenada. The Dutch recognized the independence of the United States in 1780, and helped the newborn nation with a brisk trade in munitions. In retaliation, the British West Indian fleet took over St. Eustatius and devastated the island. When all the Caribbean fighting was over, Tobago changed hands once again and was ceded to France. Florida became a Spanish possession.

THE POWDER KEG EXPLODES

Sugar was in some ways the curse of the Caribbean. The industry brought economic, political and social upheaval to the islands, much of it violent and destructive.

The Spaniards brought the first African slaves to the Caribbean in 1510 to work their mines and sugar plantations on Hispaniola. They came from West Africa. Factories were set up along the Guinea coast where African chiefs and kings brought slaves for trade. Each chief or king received a fee for each slave sold, plus a commission. First the Portuguese, then the English, Dutch and French came to fill the growing demand for the Caribbean plantations. When the trade began, a good horse would buy fifteen slaves. Later, the Africans demanded payment in their own coin, cowrie shells and certain European goods.

The Middle Passage taken by the slave ships across the Atlantic was pure hell. The slaves were crowded together in the hold, swept by small-pox and dysentery. It is conservatively estimated that six per cent of all slaves shipped during the centuries that slave trade flourished died on the Atlantic voyage.

Buyers of this human cargo in the West Indies had preferences as to tribes. The Gold Coast Negros, the Koromantyn, were tough, hard-working, brave and stubborn. From them were to come leaders of slave rebellions. From the tribes to the north and east of Sierra Leone came Mohammedan Negroes who could read and write in Arabic. They were not fitted for hard labor in the fields. Papaws from Whydah were popular as slaves because they worked hard, were skilled farmers, and were afraid of death and, consequently, submitted to discipline. The yellowish-colored Eboes from the Bight of Benin were timid and despondent, given to suicide, though they were cannibals at home. Negroes from Angola and the Congo were considered excellent mechanics, better fitted for domestic service than for work in the fields.

When the slaves were sold from ships or wharfs, every effort was made to break up friendships, families and any links with their past. The planter gave his slave, who arrived naked, a shirt, trousers, a knife, a hat and handkerchief. For the first few months after arrival, they were "seasoned" or left to adjust to the new country and the new climate.

Almost from the beginning, maroons (escaped slaves who had fled to the bush) were found on most of the major islands. In Jamaica they joined native Indians who had fled to the hills.

The brutal institution of slavery began to decline at about the time of the French Revolution. Talk of the "Rights of Man" raised whirlwinds of emotion in the Caribbean. White planters on French Saint-Domingue (now Haiti) demanded the rights to do what they pleased on the island. The slaves revolted and soon bloodshed bathed the island, with mulattoes fighting whites and blacks fighting mulattoes as well as whites. The revolutionary Jacobin party ruled in France and sent an army to enforce liberty, equality and fraternity. They fought on the side of the revolutionary slaves and proclaimed a conditional emancipation in August 1793. The French National Assembly confirmed the ruling and whites fled the island.

England and Spain went to war against revolutionary France, and England sent an expedition against Saint-Domingue, partly in fear that the slave rebellion would spread. Spread it did. The second maroon war broke out in Jamaica in 1795. The British were driven from Saint-Domingue by the military skill of Francoise-Dominique Tousaint, "L'Ouverture," first of a remarkable series of black Haitian military leaders. When war broke out between France and Spain, Toussaint raised an army of some four thousand black troops and fought the French. When the English invaded, he feared the restoration of slavery, turned against the Spaniards and fought on the side of the French Republican army. The United States sent him ships and supplies to fight the English. In 1801 he drew up a constitution for the island and named himself governor-general for life. Napoleon would not tolerate this and sent troops to the island to capture the black hero. Toussaint died in a French prison.

The blacks of the island had lost their first great leader, but never again were they to be sub-

ject to alien domination. An African-born slave, Jean Jacque Dessalines, took over as the head of the forces Toussaint had led. In 1804 he changed the name of Saint-Domingue to Haiti, which means "mountainous" in the Taino Indian language. In the same year he proclaimed himself Emperor of Haiti. After Dessalines' death in 1806, the giant Negro Henri Christophe ruled the land until his death in 1820. The southern part of Haiti was dominated by Pétion, a mulatto leader.

After the revolt of maroons and the slaves in Jamaica in 1795, the European nations could see the course they must take. Between 1804 and 1820 slave trade was abolished by Denmark, Holland, Spain and Sweden. Cuba continued to import slaves until 1865. Slaves rebelled in Barbados and again and again in Jamaica. Slavery was finally abolished in the British West Indies in 1833 and in the French colonies in 1848.

Cuba, the most cultured and prosperous of the Spanish colonies, was the last of the larger islands to ban slavery. It had a thriving economy based on sugar cane, tobacco and pig farming, all of which needed a continual import of slaves. The white minority on the island encouraged immigration from Europe and a strong, articulate, liberal element began to grow among the white Cubans. The slave trade, banned in 1817, was finally halted in 1865. Not until 1880 were provisions made for the emancipation of slaves, and in 1886 they were finally freed.

During the nineteenth century Britain tried numerous techniques of governing her West Indian colonies. Emancipation brought about wide social and political change. Three-quarters of a million people with no experience in the responsibilities of self-government or even in the planning of their own lives were set free. Land-owners became absentees. There were uprisings. Crown colony government replaced the old representative system on most of the British islands. This type of government was relatively impartial and, to a degree, paternal, and introduced needed economic development to the colonies. This interim period lasted until after World War I when the black people began to stir again with a hunger for more independence and responsibility.

After slavery was ended in the French islands, France took the wise, bold policy of integrating the colonies more closely with home, giving the islanders the freedom all Frenchmen enjoyed. Martinique, Guadeloupe and Cayenne each elected representatives to the National Assembly. For more than a century they have remained strongly tied to France, French in culture, government and politics.

FREEDOM COMES

Spain's power had waned toward the end of the nineteenth century and there were only three Spanish colonies in the West Indies—Cuba, Santo Domingo and Puerto Rico. When the slaves rose in French Saint-Domingue, they also raided across the border into Spanish Santo Domingo, a sleepy land given largely to cattle raising. Haiti ruled Santo Domingo until 1844 and hard feelings between the two lands of that island still occasionally erupt. The Haitians were expelled in 1844, and mulattoes ruled a new Dominican Republic until 1861, when Spain reoccupied that portion of Hispaniola. The land was so poor Spain promptly withdrew. Anarchy and tyranny followed. For eighteen years Ulises Heureaux was dictator. When he was assassinated in 1899 the country was bankrupt and chaos reigned.

Cuba in the nineteenth century experienced growth and change quite different from that of its neighboring islands. It was the largest and richest of the islands and had a prideful heritage and many well-educated citizens. White immigrants continued to arrive from Spain as political disorganization mounted in the mother country. Sugar production went up. The best tobacco in the world was grown on small Cuban farms, and the people had the skill that is required to cure fine tobacco. Disgusted with Spain's incompetence, white creoles in Cuba began to agitate for freedom. Spain sent out militarists to suppress the freedom-fever. Slaves revolted. The United States in 1848 offered to buy Cuba from Spain, but the offer was declined.

One of the great heroes of the Caribbean in the nineteenth century was Carlos Manuel de Cespédes, a liberal Cuban land-owner and lawyer. A junta of Cuban exiles in New York formed to support him. Cespédes declared Cuban independence at Yara in 1868. The Ten Years War that followed was distinguished more by courage than by organization, and consisted principally of bitter guerrilla fighting in the hills. Liberal spirits in the United States made gun-running and filibustering expeditions to Cuba, carrying weapons to the rebels in this war. In one such expedition fifty-three members of the crew of a U.S. ship were court-martialed and shot by their Spanish captors. Cespédes was killed in a Spanish raid. The fighting lasted ten years because Spain was in the throes of internal strife, the Carlist War. The insurgents surrendered in 1878. Slaves were emancipated in Cuba between 1880 and 1886.

The peace that followed until 1895 was uneasy. Conditions on the island were hurt even more by the American Sugar Refining Company, a United States corporation created in 1890. The company, which became known as the "Sugar Trust," controlled prices of Cuban sugar, and the prices dropped. The McKinley Tariff on sugar and tobacco imported into the U.S. also was a blow to the Cuban economy.

In 1895 another magnetic Cuban leader led a successful revolt. José Martí was both dedicated and able, and he led the Cuban junta. In the war that followed there were atrocities on both sides. Following the sinking of the battleship Maine by an explosion on a "courtesy" visit to Havana, the United States went to war against Spain. After Spain's defeat, the U.S. annexed Puerto Rico and obtained a naval base at Guantánamo in Cuba.

Today La Republica De Cuba, most populous island of the Caribbean, is a democratic socialist republic, and since 1958 has been working out its destiny under Fidel Castro. Major emphasis has been placed by the government on the development of agriculture. Oil was discovered in the 1950s. Numerous cement factories have expanded. Sugar, tobacco and minerals are still principal exports of the island.

Puerto Rico was a sleepy island when it was annexed by the United States in 1898. Fierce Caribs had initially discouraged Spanish settlement, and for centuries it had been one of the poorest Spanish colonies. Poor and backward it remained until after World War II. Under the leadership of Luis Muñoz Marín, a progressive

program to lure tourists, industry and investment was launched. Today the island vibrates with pride and progress. Puerto Rico became the first overseas commonwealth territory of the United States on July 3, 1950, when President Truman signed legislation giving Puerto Ricans power to write their own constitution and assume greater control of internal affairs. As a territory, the island has enjoyed a rising standard of living and does not have to pay federal income taxes. There is a movement for independence, but in a plebiscite in 1967 an overwhelming majority of voters voted to retain their present relationship with the United States.

The twentieth century has brought enviable happiness and prosperity to the Netherlands Antilles—Aruba, Bonair, Curaçao, Saba, St. Maarten and St. Eustatius. General suffrage and a new constitution were introduced in 1948, and on December 15, 1954, the Netherlands Antilles became an equal and autonomous co-partner in the Kingdom of the Netherlands. Two of the world's largest oil refineries are located on Curaçao and Aruba. For more than a decade these bright and beautiful Dutch islands have been attracting tourists with great success, and increasing numbers of visitors enjoy modern, luxurious and hospitable resorts.

Guadeloupe, Martinique and Cayenne form an Overseas Department of the Republic of France, a status attained on March 19, 1946. The Department has the right to appoint three deputies to the National Assembly, two members of the Senate and it is represented on the French Economic and Social Council. The economy of the islands is largely agricultural, and education is free and compulsory from six to sixteen years of age. Attractive resorts and epicurean restaurants supplement the fine beaches and the magnificent scenery of the islands as tourist attractions.

After economic unrest and riots in the 1930s, the British colonies in the Caribbean took the road to freedom. On Jamaica and Trinidad, the largest of these islands, universal adult suffrage was introduced under constitutions in 1944. They attained independence in 1962, and are members of the British Commonwealth of Nations. They joined the Organization of American States (OAS) in June, 1969. Both are also members of the United Nations and the Caribbean Free Trade Associations. Trinidad and Tobago are united under one government.

Most of the smaller islands that were formerly colonies of Great Britain, such as Antigua, obtained new constitutions leading to self-governing status in 1966 and are now States in Association with the United Kingdom, with full internal self-government. Other small islands, such as Montserrat and the Cayman Islands, are still British colonies. There, after negotiation conducted during 1966, the islanders elected not to move into the status of self-government.

Today these islands are new frontiers, where pioneers are learning to trust their own strength, courage and good sense. They are mastering the arts of politics and hospitality. The alluring fragrance of new-found freedom is being carried by the trade winds across the green peaks and white beaches. There is a special lilt of life on these islands.

PIRATES OF THE SPANISH MAIN

Like hawks they swooped about the Caribbean for three centuries, the pirates who enriched the beautiful region with legends of treasures. In myth they are dashing and bold but in fact, many were cruel, dirty villains.

Plundering upon the sea in the New World began almost as soon as the lumbering Spanish galleons began carrying gold, silver and emeralds back to Spain. The great gold treasures of the Americas were found in four mining centers—two in Mexico, one in Peru, and one, the fabled Postosi mine, in Bolivia. The Pope had divided the non-Christian world between Spain and Portugal. Portugal was given Africa with its fortune in slaving. Spain was given the western world with its riches in gold. The Protestant nations of Europe did not recognize the legality of this partition of the globe.

Privateers and pirates began to swarm to the Caribbean. Privateers only attacked and plundered their country's enemies. They fitted out their ships at their own expense, were granted letters of marque by their kings and queens, and shared their loot with the crown. Pirates attacked anyone, and were men without allegiance to any nation.

First of these sea-raiders were the French corsairs who began to raid the Spanish galleons when Francis I was king. Before he was beheaded by the Spanish, Jean Florin confessed that he had robbed and sunk one hundred and fifty Spanish ships. In 1555 Captain François le Clerk, "Pegleg," led French corsairs who sacked Havana and held the rich for ransom.

John Hawkins was initially a slave smuggler and a privateer, one of the first of those encouraged by Queen Elizabeth when she came to the English throne in 1558. She knighted him, as she did Sir Francis Drake who began his career as the captain of one of Hawkins' small ships. Drake sailed in glory when he went raiding Her Majesty's enemies around the world from 1577 to 1580. Victorious in raids on Santo Domingo, Havana, Cartagena, Panama and St. Augustine in Florida, Drake never considered himself reprehensible. His fighting was against England's foes.

"The Brotherhood of the Coast" was the name of that group of buccaneers who camped on the western end of Hispaniola. They dried strips of meat by smoking them over a slow fire called "boucan," and thence the name "buccaneers." They were shipwrecked sailors, deserters, criminals, adventurers, free spirits. From the buccaneers, pirate crews were recruited.

Tortuga, an island just north of Hispaniola, was an early haunt of international buccaneers in the seventeenth century. English buccaneers headquartered at Port Royal in Jamaica with the approval of Jamaica's governors. From this stronghold Henry Morgan sacked the Spanish Main. He died in 1688 as lieutenant-governor of Jamaica. Port Royal perished in an earthquake in 1692 when it sank beneath the sea.

Captain William Kidd was a respected ship captain in New York when he was sent by England to wipe out pirates in the Indian ocean. He turned pirate himself and looted ships from the East Indies to the Caribbean. His infamy lived on long after he was captured and hanged in London in 1701.

Another of the more famous pirates was Edward Teach, called Blackbeard. He was a huge, fierce man with a black beard that reached almost to his waist. Blackbeard's hideaway was in St. Thomas in the Virgin Islands, until he began to headquarter on New Providence Island in the Bahamas. It was purported that he had an alliance with Governor Charles Eden of North Carolina. Teach was killed off the Outer Banks of North Carolina by Lieutenant Robert Maynard of the Royal Navy.

The honor of sweeping the last of the Caribbean pirates from the sea goes to the United States Navy under the command of Commodore David Porter in the 1820s. With England's aid and an appropriation from Congress of $500,000, Porter outfitted his squadron. He captured scores of pirate ships from his base in Key West and by 1830 the Jolly Roger flew no more.

THE PEOPLE OF THE CARIBBEAN

Throughout the islands today there is an exciting mixture of different ethnic strains from all over the world—African, European, Oriental, Indian. The original natives, Arawaks and Caribs, were all but exterminated. Aruba is one of the few islands on which a sizeable Indian population remained for some centuries after white men arrived. There the high cheekbones, the straight black hair and the friendliness of the Arawaks can be seen in many hospitable Arubans. In most of the islands the black people who were brought in chains from Africa are in the majority, and they are inheriting that beautiful earth.

There is a great deal of difference among the black people. Many islanders, of course, have considerable white blood. But among the Africans who seem to have undiluted Negro ancestry there are distinct differences in face and physique. This is not surprising, since Africa is a land of many different and distinct tribes, from the Mohammedan Negroes in the north of the continent, with their silky hair and aquiline features, to the powerful big, black men from the Congo.

Attitudes of masters toward their slaves shaped the future that is being born today. Many freed their illegitimate offspring, children of their slaves. Slaves could also, under Spanish law, buy their freedom or win it by saving their master's life. Almost from the beginning there were a number of free Negroes and many free mulattoes. They formed a separate caste or class, above the Negro slaves, below the white slave-owner. White blood, as evidenced by light brown color, was more desirable than black.

Today, on many of the newly independent islands, this is not true. In some parts of the Caribbean it is easier for a black man to get a job or hold a political post than it is for a mulatto, and far easier than it is for a white man. This is particularly true in the islands that once were English colonies, for the English considered their slaves property, not people. They drew a line that shut blacks out of their world, and now white men are leaving Jamaica and Trinidad, as a line shutting them out of the dominant black world is being drawn.

The French were different. French soldiers fought beside black slaves against white slave-owners in Saint Domingue during the French Revolution. The women of Martinique, white and black, for some centuries have been famous for their beauty.

The easiest race relations, over the centuries, have developed between blacks and whites in what were once Spanish colonies, because the Spanish were the most humane. In the islands where the Spanish influence dominated, color lines were not drawn so sharply and arbitrarily. There is a mixing, and an easier, more equal, feeling among people of all colors.

The Africans who were brought to the New World did not retain their languages. They learned English, Spanish, French or Dutch. Whole new languages were developed, like the Papiamento of Aruba and Curaçao, which is a mixture of Spanish, Portuguese and Dutch, with some Arawak and English words. The slaves brought a musical lilt in their speech, which they gave to the languages they adopted. They brought their gods of Africa, and their magic, Obeah, which still lives throughout the Caribbean. Many still believe as devoutly in the witch-doctors who treat them as in the churches they may attend. They brought voodoo, which is still practiced in Haiti.

When the slave trade ended, the plantation owners were desperate for labor, many East Indians and Chinese came to the Caribbean in the last century to work as indentured laborers on five-year contracts. A considerable number of Chinese coolies were brought into Cuba. Many stayed. The Chinese became shopkeepers. It is not unusual to see Oriental features in boys and girls born in the Antilles.

Along with freedom and the right to govern themselves, the people of the Caribbean have also acquired the responsibility for their own economy. This has resulted in a major new industry—tourism—that has supplanted sugar cane on many of the islands. Puerto Rico and Jamaica set the pace after World War II. Sunseekers from North and South America and Europe began to flock to this beautiful world. Resort hotels and attractive accommodations were built. The people could see that tourism produced more jobs than other major industries. Learning the arts of professional hospitality has come easy to Caribbean islanders, because they are by nature a fun-loving people with a positive preference for happiness.

All through the islands new resorts are being built. Yachtsmen find new hideaways, adventurers come back with tales of beautiful beaches and exotic rain forests. Though the black people who are in the majority draw the line at letting white people run their world, they are gracious and easy-going with their guests. There is a spontaneous, whole-hearted joy of life that pervades this world, even though living may often be bitterly hard and the people poor.

GEOLOGY

Volcanos, coral reefs and mangrove trees have been the land-builders of the Caribbean. The volcanic upheavals that first thrust the rocky islands above the sea began about seventy million years ago in the Cretaceous Period, when the first reptiles and insects were appearing on the earth. In between volcanic periods the sea rose and many of the islands were buried under thick layers of limestone.

The first upheavals created the mountainous backbone of Mexico and Central America and two chains of mountains extending east into the Caribbean were formed. One reached what is now Jamaica, and the other extended through Cuba, Hispaniola and Puerto Rico to the Virgin Islands. In the south, Trinidad and Barbados appeared above the sea. For millions of years afterward the volcanoes were quiet and thick deposits of marine sediments were formed. Volcanoes that created some of the islands—Anguilla, St. Martin, St. Barthélemy, Antigua, Désirade, Marie Galante and part of Guadeloupe—are no longer active.

About twenty-five million years ago, in Late Miocene and early Pliocene times, the world went through another great volcanic period. At that time the inner volcanic chain of the Lesser Antilles, from Saba in the north to Grenada in the south, was formed. Oil was deposited at Trinidad and bauxite in Jamaica during that period.

Today there is occasional volcanic activity on three islands in the Lesser Antilles—St. Vincent, Guadeloupe and Martinique. The fault that causes earthquakes in the Caribbean has caused many destructive quakes. Jamaica, the Windward Islands, Cap Haitien, Port-au-Prince and the Virgin Islands have experienced earthquakes.

The highest mountain in the region is a 10,000-foot peak in the Dominican Republic. Few of the mountainous islands are more than 7,000 feet high. The folding that produced the mountains also made enormous sea troughs. The deep groove called the Bartlett Trough extends for a thousand miles between Cuba and Jamaica, and is more than 20,000 feet deep in places. The Brownson

Trough north of Puerto Rico and the Virgin Islands is even deeper. In this, the deepest part of the Atlantic, Mount Everest could get lost. the smaller Anegada Trough separates the Virgin Islands and Puerto Rico from the Lesser Antilles and St. Croix and is the only deep-water channel between the Atlantic and the Caribbean.

Since the last Ice Age the many-rooted mangrove trees have extended the coastal flats around the islands. Their seeds are viable in salt water, sprout on sand-bars and shores, and trap sand and mud around their roots to build more land.

Coral reefs have contributed beaches and beauty to the islands they surround. The great reef-building corals of the tropics are minute animals that take calcium carbonate from sea water to build their rock-like homes. The rocks remain when the corals die, and more corals build upon them. Barrier reefs, fringing reefs and bank reefs all are found off-shore in the Caribbean. They are home to a multitude of fishes that hide among them, and they contribute snow-white sand to the beaches as they erode. They make magnificent undersea scenery.

CLIMATE

The Caribbean islands are air-conditioned by the equable trade winds that blow from the Atlantic. The easterly trades dominate the wind patterns and moderate the climate. Columbus was the first navigator to report on the prevailing trade winds that followed his ships from Spain to the New World. These winds circulate around a high pressure area in the North Atlantic ocean that lies between Bermuda and the Azores islands. South of this high pressure system the winds blow from the east, and north of it they blow from the west.

Benign temperatures accompany these winds throughout the region which stretches from the Bahamas to South America and from Barbados to Central America. The average temperature of the hottest months is 80°F, and the coolest winter months seldom have an average temperature below 75°F. The temperature of the surrounding waters varies little from summer to winter.

There is a refreshing range of temperature from day to night. While midday temperatures may climb above 90°F even in cooler months, they drop refreshingly at night to 70° in the Lesser Antilles and 65° in the Greater Antilles. The high peaks thrusting from the Caribbean offer a pleasant change. The temperature drops an average of one degree for every three hundred feet of elevation and some of the highest peaks can be chilly.

The breezes that bathe the islands are moist and carry puffy white cumulus clouds across the blue sky. Though moist, they do not tend to produce long rainy days, but rather heavy, brief showers. All of the islands have a rainy season and one season that is fairly dry, which is typical of the Tropical Marine climate they enjoy.

Because the high pressure areas over the North and South Atlantic shift as the seasons change, the equatorial rain belt moves north and south. This rain belt is produced where the Northeast Trades of the North Atlantic and the Southeast Trades of the South Atlantic converge. In January the rain belt lies along the equator. It begins to move north in May and reaches as high as 15°N. latitude in August, retreating southward slowly thereafter. This shifting rain belt brings the heaviest rainfall while it is overhead, and thus the islands fartherest north have their wet season later in the summer than do those farther south.

The rainfall pattern of the Greater Antilles differs from that of the Lesser Antilles because these islands are big and their mountains are high. Many of the peaks are bathed in clouds which stream to windward. The winds rise as they approach the peaks, the rising air cools, big clouds form and the rain falls. The pattern is such that the land on the side from which the wind blows receives heavy rains, and the peaks become rain forests, while on the leeward side of the peaks the land lies in a "rain shadow," and only receives a light rainfall. On smaller islands the rain clouds may blow over the peaks and fall on the leeward coasts. The smaller, lower islands are drier than the larger, higher ones with their cloud-bathed peaks.

The convectional rainfall that drenches the coasts of the islands of the Greater Antilles has a particular pattern. The land heats more quickly than the surrounding sea, and rising currents of air are formed as the trade winds reach the mountain slopes. By noon clouds have formed as the rising air cools. Late in the afternoon the clouds shadow the land, the convection currents cease to form, and rain, with thunder and lightning, comes pouring down. Because the land cools more quickly than the sea, in the evening a land breeze blows seaward, skies are clear and nights are cool.

Troughs of low atmospheric pressure move through the area from east to west, principally between June and November. They bring the rainy season to the Lesser Antilles. Hurricanes are born occasionally from these low pressure areas in the Atlantic and the Caribbean, and may sweep from the Lesser Antilles to New England, causing great damage. A most beautiful phenomenon associated with hurricanes is the magnificent sunsets that precede them. Scattered cirrus and cumulus clouds ride high before the rains, and the heavens may become gold and rose and green and pink from west to east as the setting sun plays upon the broken cloud cover.

VEGETATION

The mantle of green and the fragrance of flowers enchanted the first explorers of the Antilles, just as they delight today's visitors. But the vegetation has changed since Columbus first saw the islands almost five hundred years ago. Because many forests have been cut and many magnificent trees,

shrubs and flowering plants have been introduced, the West Indian vegetation is quite different from that found by the early colonists.

The climate makes for a year round growing season, but the air grows cooler as the mountains rise. The amount of rain varies, and the character of the soils differs, and this makes for different landscapes on each island. There are islands with a landscape like that of Arizona, rolling, dry and cactus-studded. Other islands have tropical rain-forests and elfin woodlands on their high peaks, and there the lush green trees have exotic orchids and ferns hanging from them. Mangroves grow along the shores of all the islands that have shallow coastal waters. They build land and prevent erosion of the coasts by trapping sand and silt in their dense nets of roots. Coconut palms, almost all planted by man, grace the beaches. Handsome native sea-grape trees thrive in the salt air and the sea spray.

The tropical rain-forests of the wet lowland areas is a treasure house for plant lovers. A great variety of tall and handsome broad-leaved trees are found there. The trees become smaller as the forests climb the mountains, and orchids, bromeliads and ferns become more numerous. The gnarled and dense woodlands on the mist-enshrouded mountain peaks have a magic about them. Broad savannahs, tropical grasslands, are found throughout the West Indies, some made by man through cultivation, others a result of natural conditions. Most of the original forests have been cleared to obtain timber and to raise crops. Certain of the forests that remain are now reserves

and clearing is prohibited. Following cultivation, considerable land is being reforested in certain areas.

Among the plants that the Indians were cultivating when the Spaniards first arrived were pumpkins, corn, potatoes, yams, tomatoes, squash, peanuts, cassava plants, cotton, pineapples, beans and tobacco. Avocado trees are native to Central America. The islands have proved hospitable to a great variety of introduced agricultural plants and trees—sugar cane, bananas, oranges, coffee trees, mangoes, grape vines, rice and breadfruit.

Flowering shrubs and trees are even more numerous. Most than a hundred species of hibiscus are planted for ornamental purposes, and their blooms may be red, yellow, pink or white. The royal poinciana tree that flames into an orange bloom is a breath-taking sight. Shaving brushes grow on trees (the Bombax ellipticum). Poinsettias, red and white, enrich the landscape. The pink poui tree, the candle bush, the red bottle brush tree, the flame of the forest (African tulip tree)— their names suggest their exotic beauty. The night-blooming cereus, flower of a cactus-like vine, is unforgettable. The oldest botanical garden in the region is on St. Vincent Island and is over two hundred years old.

PUERTO RICO

A self-governing commonwealth within the U.S.A., Puerto Rico is rich in beautiful scenery, magnificent beaches, mountains more than 4,300 ft. high and lush forests. It has excellent roads, first rate hotels, legal gambling. The capital, San Juan, is a large commercial metropolis with well preserved historical quarters. There are direct airline connections with numerous U.S. cities, Canada, Europe, other Caribbean islands and Central and South America. Visitors enjoy horse racing, many fine golf courses, tennis, hunting, horseback riding, water skiing, sailing, fishing (sailfish, marlin, dolphin, kingfish, tuna and bonito). Puerto Rico covers 3,423 square miles. The population is approximately 2,800,000 Spanish and English are the principal languages. Approximately 1,850,000 visitors arrive annually, and of these 450,000 come on cruise ships. The annual average temperature is 78° F.

Puerto Rico is a place where people love to live because it has fine mountains, a warm, crystal-clear sea, spectacular beauty and a kind climate. However, for centuries after it was discovered in 1493, the island was poor and life hard for most people. Juan Ponce de León settled this land in 1508. It was a possession of Spain until the Spanish-American War. Puerto Rico became a United States territory under the Treaty of Paris in 1899.

For decades thereafter the island was poor. Today Puerto Rico is an inspiration to the other Antillean islands, thanks to Operation Bootstrap, an inspiration of former Governor Muñoz Marin. He once said, "We must live like angels and produce like devils." He designed a program to court industry and tourists that has been wondrously successful. Tax advantages have lured more than five hundred new industries, which range from small textile plants to a huge Union Carbide plant. The tourist industry is ever-expanding.

Puerto Rico is one hundred miles long and forty miles wide. The most easterly of the larger islands of the West Indies, it rises beside the waters of the Brownson Deep, which go down 7,000 feet below the surface. The highest mountain peak, Cerro de Punta in the central part of the island, rises to 4,398 feet. The climate is practically perfect, for the island is far enough north to escape oppressive tropical heat, and the trade winds cool the land. There are miles of fine beaches, wide fertile plains and splendid forests filled with ferns and flowers, such as the Caribbean National Forest on the slopes of Luquillo Mountains.

Ponce de León gave the island its name, which literally means rich or beautiful port. San Juan is the capital city. The warring European powers—Spain, France, England, and Holland—fought over Puerto Rico from time to time. Massive fortresses were built by the Spanish to protect the harbor. Luis Muñoz Rivera, Puerto Rico's George Washington, won dominion status for the island from Spain in 1897. Two years later Puerto Rico became the first "colony" of the United States. The islanders became American citizens in 1917, and they voted to establish the self-governing Commonwealth of Puerto Rico in 1952.

San Juan is an enchanting city. The Old City is Spanish colonial in style, with great forts and narrow streets. Built on an island, it is today linked by causeway and by bridges to the mainland. Under the Old City is a network of tunnels that once linked strategic places, but it is now closed.

Continued on page 44

Descriptions of the following pictures

page 25
PUERTO RICO: LUQUILLO BEACH
A few miles east of San Juan is the magnificent, popular beach, Luquillo. It ranks among the most beautiful beaches in the world: crescent-shaped, covered with fine white sand, surrounded by a forest of coconut palms. The waters are calm, clear, blue-green in color. It is well-kept by the Puerto Rican government.

page 26
OLD SAN JUAN, PUERTO RICO
This air view from the north is especially interesting because it shows the fortification of the Old City: Morro Castle to the far right, the city walls running along the northern coast of the island leading to Castillo de San Cristóbal. Some parts of the wall and La Fortaleza on the southern waterfront are also visible. In the background is the entrance to the harbor of San Juan.

FAST-GROWING MODERN SAN JUAN
One of the fastest growing modern cities in the U.S.A. and one of the largest (455,000 population) in the Caribbean islands, San Juan attained its present elegant appearance in less than two decades. The picture shows a small part of the great new city, the Condado section with many new apartment houses and hotels along a beautiful beach.

PONCE: R. C. CATHEDRAL, PUERTO RICO
The second largest city of Puerto Rico, with a population of approximately 180,000, Ponce was founded in 1692, seventy-six miles southwest of San Juan on the south coast of the island. The romantic Spanish flavor of this city has been beautifully preserved. In the center of town is the Cathedral of Our Lady of Guadeloupe, which separates two lovely plazuelas and dominates one.

page 27
OLD SAN JUAN: CASTILLO DE SAN FELIPE DEL MORRO, PUERTO RICO
This great fortress is the chief tourist attraction of Old San Juan. Built by the Spanish at the northwest end of the city from 1539 to 1586, it covers more than two hundred acres and rises 145 feet above the ocean. The castle was continuously improved until 1787. It is now a National Historic Site.

page 28
TRUNK BAY, ST. JOHN, U.S. VIRGIN ISLANDS
Once the richest of the Virgins, with 109 estates, St. John is today a quiet, secluded island, an escapist's paradise, for most of the early inhabitants died in a slave revolt in 1733. A large part of the island is a National Park. Jungle overgrew the old estates, and today one sees green mountains, sandy bays, deep valleys, sparkling water and white sand beaches. One of the thirty-one bays with a beautiful beach is Trunk Bay, with clear, calm waters, perfect for snorkelers and divers.

page 29
CRUISE SHIPS IN ST. THOMAS HARBOR
The most popular cruise stop in the Caribbean, sometimes there are up to twelve ships in picturesque St. Thomas Harbor. With good reasons: It's a very safe harbor, the scenery is great, and sightseeing is worthwhile. The main reason for most tourists, however, is the unique freeport shopping that offers a wide choice of merchandise, with permission to bring $200 worth of it into the United States duty free.

page 29
HARBOR OF ST. THOMAS, U.S. VIRGIN ISLANDS
Approaching St. Thomas by air from the northwest, this beautiful view opens into the harbor, with Charlotte Amalie, the capital, in the background. To the right is Water Island.

page 30
CHRISTIANSTED, ST. CROIX, U.S. VIRGIN ISLANDS
This well-preserved Danish port was for many years capital of the Danish Virgin Islands. With its romantic streets and interesting historical buildings painted in pastel colors, it is one of the highlights of every Caribbean visit.

Continued on page 41

PUERTO RICO: LUQUILLO BEACH

OLD SAN JUAN
FROM THE NORTH

PUERTO RICO

For detailed description see page 24

MODERN SAN JUAN,
CONDADO SECTION

PONCE: THE ROMAN
CATHOLIC CATHEDRAL

OLD SAN JUAN: CASTILLO DE SAN FELIPE DEL MORRO

U.S. VIRGIN ISLANDS

←

TRUNK BAY, ST. JOHN

*CRUISE SHIPS IN
ST. THOMAS HARBOR*

ST. THOMAS HARBOR

ST. CROIX
U.S. VIRGIN ISLANDS

CHRISTIANSTED

*SAILS ON
PROTESTANT CAY*

*FOUNTAIN VALLEY
GOLF COURSE*

30

BEACH AT CANEEL BAY,
ST. JOHN, U.S. VIRGIN ISLANDS

CHARLOTTE AMALIE
FROM
BLUEBEARD'S CASTLE

ST. THOMAS
U.S. VIRGIN ISLANDS

SAPPHIRE BAY

EASTERN ST. JOHN: HURRICANE HOLE AND ROUND BAY
U.S. VIRGIN ISLANDS

ROAD TOWN, TORTOLA

BRITISH VIRGIN ISLANDS

THE BATHS, VIRGIN GORDA (BRIT. VIRGIN ISLANDS)

32

UNDERWATER TRAIL, BUCK ISLAND REEF NATIONAL MONUMENT

BUCK ISLAND (ST. CROIX)
U.S. VIRGIN ISLANDS

DIVING THE WRECK
OF R.M.S. RHONE
OFF SALT ISLAND,
BRIT. VIRGIN ISLANDS

BEACH, MULLET BAY

ST. MAARTEN

ON GREAT BAY

VIEW OVER PHILIPSBURG
FROM FORT WILLIAM

ST. MAARTEN

For detailed description see page 42

MULLET BAY
18-HOLE
GOLF COURSE

ON THE BEACH
OF LITTLE BAY

ST. EUSTATIUS (STATIA)

For detailed description see page 42

SABA

*BOTTOM, THE CAPITAL
OF SABA*

36

LOOKING OVER ST. KITTS (ST. CHRISTOPHER)

AIR VIEW OF ST. BARTHELEMY

MONTSERRAT: CAPITAL PLYMOUTH WITH SOUFRIERE (3002 FT.)

ANTIGUA: HISTORICAL ENGLISH HARBOUR →

ST. JOHN'S
CAPITAL OF ANTIGUA

ANTIGUA

For detailed description see page 43

LONG BAY, ONE OF
THE MANY BEAUTIFUL
BEACHES OF ANTIGUA

CARNIVAL IN ANTIGUA

TYPICAL COUNTRYSIDE SCENE

40

Description of foregoing pictures -
continued from page 24

page 30
SAILBOATS ON PROTESTANT CAY, ST. CROIX
Little Protestant Cay facing Christiansted offers a colorful choice of sailboats (catamarans) for trips around the island.

FOUNTAIN VALLEY GOLF COURSE, ST. CROIX, U.S. VIRGIN ISLANDS
One of the outstanding golf courses in the world, this eighteen-hole course designed by Robert Trent Jones lies in a beautiful setting dotted with flowering trees in the northern hills of the island. A luncheon terrace and bar overlook the valley and golf course, which has a pro shop and equipment rentals.

page 31
BEACH AT CANEEL BAY, ST. JOHN, U.S. VIRGIN ISLANDS
The Virgin Islands are filled with secluded beaches like the one pictured here. The sands are powder soft, the waters translucent blue or green, marvelous for skin-diving and underwater exploration. At Caneel Bay on the quiet island of St. John is one of the outstanding resorts, Caneel Bay Plantation, built with all modern conveniences into the ruins of an ancient Danish plantation.

CHARLOTTE AMALIE, VIEW FROM BLUEBEARD'S CASTLE, ST. THOMAS, U.S. VIRGIN ISLANDS
One of the great views of St. Thomas: As we look down from the terrace of Bluebeard's Castle, the harbor of St. Thomas and the city of Charlotte Amalie surround us with a unique setting. To the right is Charlotte Amalie; in the background French Town and Water Island. In front is a Royal Poinciana tree in full bloom, a glory of the Caribbean.

SAPPHIRE BAY, ST. THOMAS, U.S. VIRGIN ISLANDS
One of many beautiful beaches of St. Thomas is at Sapphire Bay, framed by sea grape trees and coconut palms.

page 32
EASTERN ST. JOHN, U.S. VIRGIN ISLANDS
The air view shows the most eastern part of St. John looking down on Hurricane Hole in the foreground, behind Round Bay, to the right Coral Bay, to the left The Narrows.

BRITISH VIRGIN ISLANDS
Looking down from a plane, the photograph shows Road Town, Tortola, capital of the British Virgin Islands. The lower picture was taken in The Baths, an interesting grotto on the coast of Virgin Gorda, consisting of three caves, washed by the sea over fine white sand. The light effects there are very dramatic.

page 33
BUCK ISLAND REEF NATIONAL MONUMENT, ST. CROIX, U.S. VIRGIN ISLANDS
This island, just off the coast of St. Croix, was designated a National Monument because of the barrier reef that surrounds the eastern part of it. In the clear lagoon between the island and the reef are remarkable formations of elkhorn, staghorn and brain coral, with colorful fish and other interesting marine life. Buck Island, just a mile long and about 300 feet high, is easily reached from Christiansted.

DIVING THE WRECK OF R.M.S. RHONE OFF SALT ISLAND
A diver explores the skeleton of a sunken ship, which is completely overgrown with many species of sponges and a few gorgonians. It is the wreck of the British mail ship "Rhone", which sank in a storm in 1867 off Salt Island east of St. John, Virgin Islands. She is 360 ft. long and lies in 35 to 80 ft. of water. There are many ship wrecks around the Virgins, especially Anegada, British Virgin Islands.

page 34
BEACH, MULLET BAY, ST. MAARTEN
On the Dutch side of the island along the south coast is a string of magnificent beaches: Little Bay, Great Bay, Simson Bay, Maho Bay. Close to the French border is Mullet Bay, with a beautiful beach and resort, where this picture was taken.

ON GREAT BAY, ST. MAARTEN
Looking down from a plane on the Dutch portion of this island shows a view of Great Bay in the foreground. In the background to the right is the Great Salt Pond with the green mountains of Dutch Cul-de-Sac.

page 35
VIEW FROM FORT WILLIAM OVER PHILIPSBURG, ST. MAARTEN
West of Philipsburg, capital of Dutch St. Maarten, on a hill is ancient Fort William with an excellent view over Philipsburg, the Great Salt Pond to the left and Great Bay to the right.

MULLET BAY 18-HOLE GOLF COURSE
One of the most delightful developments of St. Maarten is Mullet Bay with this attractive eighteen hole golf course close to a beautiful beach and hotel.

ON THE BEACH OF LITTLE BAY, ST. MAARTEN
Little Bay offers one of the most beautiful sandy beaches in Dutch St. Maarten. There is the Little Bay Beach Hotel, with more than 100 rooms and an attractive gambling casino.

page 36
ST. EUSTATIUS (STATIA)
This Dutch island was once the most important trading center in the Caribbean. It was of great assistance to the American Revolution, and from Fort Oranje the first foreign salute to the U.S. flag was fired on November 16, 1776. For this act it was sacked by Great Britain and the capital, Oranjestad, completely destroyed in 1781. There is now an airport, the hotel "Golden Era," and two guest houses on the island. Windward Islands Airways connects it with St. Maarten by a short flight.

SABA
This imposing volcanic rock rising from the Caribbean is five square miles in size, 2,900 feet in height, and one of the most memorable specks of land in the West Indies. Saba, which is Dutch, has several villages, but no harbor, no sandy beach.

There is a landing strip, Yrausquin Airport, on its northeast corner. There are good accommodations for tourists on the island. The heart of this strangely beautiful island is cool, fresh and green. Mt. Scenery (2,900 ft.), seen in the photograph, is the highest peak on the island and the highest mountain in the Netherlands Antilles.

THE CAPITAL TOWN OF SABA, BOTTOM WITH MOUNTAIN ROAD TO WINDWARDSIDE
Overlooking the fertile valley and village of Bottom with the residence of the administrator of the island, the picture shows also the wild romantic road up to St. John's Hill leading to the other larger village of Windwardside, about 800 feet higher than Bottom. The pleasantly cool temperatures in Saba, exposed to the cooling tradewinds result in the freshly green vegetation, visible in the picture.

page 37
LOOKING OVER ST. KITTS (ST. CHRISTOPHER)
A view from the ramparts of Brimstone Hill Fort, St. Christopher's mighty fortification, shows in the far distance the silhouette of St. Eustatius and in the foreground the fertile land of St. Kitts. The island's economy is still based mainly on sugar cane production and vast, well-cultivated cane fields cover most of the island. There is also commercial fishing. Tourism is developing slowly, and there are fine beaches and attractive scenery. Small hotels and guest houses take care of the visitors.

AIR VIEW OF ST. BARTHÉLEMY (ST. BARTS)
The photograph shows the western part of the quaint island and the capital, Gustavia, with the finest harbor in the Caribbean. Measuring only eight square miles, it has a population of about 2,400, mostly descendants of Frenchmen who came to the island in the seventeenth century from Normandy, Brittany and Poitou. The French were the first to colonize St. Barts, but in 1784 they ceded it to Sweden in return for trading rights in Goetheborg. It was returned to France in 1877, but during the period of Swedish rule its capital had acquired the name Gustavia, for Gustavus III, and this is still its name.

page 38
MONTSERRAT: CAPITAL PLYMOUTH WITH SUFFRIERE (3,002 FEET)

Looking from the west to the green mountains of Montserrat, Plymouth, the capital, is in the foreground. This is a lively city with government offices, a few small hotels and good theater, in addition to the usual local entertainment of calypso and steel bands. Montserrat is one of the most beautiful, unspoiled islands of the Caribbean. Covered with green forests with clear streams and waterfalls, it has marvelous drinking water and a plentiful supply of it. When other islands suffer from drought, Montserrat sends shiploads of crystal clear water. It is called the Emerald Isle, both because of its rich green appearance and also for its first settlers, who came from Ireland. A shamrock adorns the gable of the Government House.

page 39
ANTIGUA: HISTORICAL ENGLISH HARBOUR

One of the spectacular attractions of Antigua is English Harbour, where Lord Nelson labored to prepare his fleet, which in time destroyed Napoleon's sea-power at Trafalgar. English Harbour, a chain of bays reaching deep into the island, offered a perfect hideaway for the British fleet. As you pass through the dockyard gates you have the impression of stepping into the late eighteenth century; old cannons, anchors, sun dials and caldrons for boiling pitch abound. The entire area is alive with memories of Antigua's exciting and romantic past.

page 40
ST. JOHN'S, CAPITAL OF ANTIGUA

The picture shows St. John's, capital of Antigua, an attractive little city in the northwestern part of the island. The government offices, the ministries, the court house, the seat of Parliament and the Cathedral are in St. John's.

LONG BAY, ANTIGUA

Antigua is rich with beautiful beaches. One of them is Long Bay, seen from the Long Bay Hotel. In the background is the Horizons Hotel. Horseback riding is popular in Antigua.

TYPICAL COUNTRYSIDE SCENE, ANTIGUA

A sugar mill ruin, the native woman with her basket on her head, the children astride the mule could have been photographed anywhere in Antigua.

CARNIVAL IN ANTIGUA

One of the great summer festivals of the island is Carnival, celebrated the week before the first Monday in August. The color, noise and vigor compare favorably with other famous pre-Lenten Carnivals. The greatest days are the four last ones, with ten thousands of visitors arriving from the neighboring islands. There are parades in most unusual costumes, side shows, calypso and steelbands, crowning of a Carnival Queen, parading of the previous "Royal Family," dancers and clowns—an annual escape for emotions and energies. It is a loud and colorful affair, full of original ideas and art and plenty of music.

Continued from page 23

In the Old City of San Juan the historical landmarks include Castillo de San Felipe del Morro. Completed in 1586, this fort covers more than two hundred acres. The Fortaleza was rebuilt in 1640, and is half-fort, half-palace. Today it is the official residence of the Governor of Puerto Rico. Near the seaside gardens of this beautiful estate is the Cathedral of St. John the Baptist, where the bones of Ponce de León lie. One of the oldest churches in the Western Hemisphere is the Church of San José, built in 1523. A bronze statue of Ponce de León forged from captured cannons dominates the Plaza nearby.

Other places to visit in the Old City are the Casa Blanca, which was built as a home for Ponce de León in 1523, and El Convento, a seventeenth century convent for Carmelite nuns which has been converted into an attractive hotel. Another massive fortress, San Cristobal, commands the eastern approaches to the harbor.

There is also much that is new and attractive in and around San Juan. The horse race track, Hipodromo de El Comandante, is one of the prettiest in the world. A pleasure park beside the sea, Parque Muñoz Rivera, overlooks a baseball stadium. The stately Capitol, the Supreme Court building, the University of Puerto Rico at Rio Piedras are all handsome and interesting modern buildings.

Sight-seeing is pleasant in Puerto Rico, not only because the sights are so beautiful but also because the island has more than three thousand miles of excellent roads. The Condado section on the outskirts of San Juan has the luxurious resort hotels. Palm-shaded Luquillo Beach is one of the most beautiful in the Caribbean. El Yunque, the tropical rain forest that is the Caribbean National Forest, is on a mountain slope less than an hour's drive from San Juan.

Ponce, the second largest city on the island, offers many pleasures. Colonial Spain is quite as

Puerto Rico

ATLANTIC OCEAN

CARIBBEAN SEA

much in evidence as in San Juan, but in a different style. Here there are colonial mansions, romantic walled patios, balconies overlooking flowering gardens. A red and black striped building was once the Ponce firehouse. The Cathedral of Our Lady of Guadaloupe is serene. This city, with its two lovely plazas, proves that the Spaniards had a fine sense of how to design a city for human pleasure. Today luxurious resort hotels in Ponce offer all the amenities to tourists. Outstanding is the Ponce Museum of Art, a modern building with an excellent collection of paintings.

On the western tip of Puerto Rico is Mayagüez, which is the island's third largest city. Here an agricultural experiment station is said to have the largest collection of tropical plants in the Western Hemisphere. This is an important port city. Artists with needle and thread have made Mayagüez famous for embroidery and needlework.

A drive along the coast leads to La Parguera and "The Bay of Living Light." The phosphorescence in the waters at night is almost bright enough to read by. Continuing north is the ancient town of San German. Founded by Diego Columbus, here the Porta Coeli Church was built in 1513.

"Portorriquenos," as the islanders call themselves, are a musical people. Great musical artists of the world appear at the three-week musical festival held in the spring. It has been shaped around the gifted cellist Pablo Casals. The islanders and their visitors also enjoy symphony concerts, opera, ballet and theater.

Visitors to Puerto Rico need never be at a loss for things to do. Night-life is fascinating and sophisticated, with entertainment, gambling casinos, fine restaurants and dancing. During the day, deepsea fishing, shore fishing and lake fishing reward anglers. There are facilities for all sorts of water sports; water skiing, skin-diving and sailing. Golfers have many choices among excellent courses. Puerto Rico is a rich port, indeed.

THE VIRGIN ISLANDS

A group of jagged rocks on the horizon covered with spray and mist like wisps of veils, reminded Columbus of a giant frieze of kneeling women. He thought of St. Ursula and her eleven thousand virgins awaiting martyrdom and he called the rocky islands the Virgins. These volcanic cones, inactive for millennia, loom to heights of 1,500 feet above the sea. They are located just east of Puerto Rico on the rim of the Antilles beside the Atlantic. They include three small islands, St. Thomas, St. Croix and St. John, and some forty-eight smaller islands and cays.

The history of the Virgins is unique. These islands were the northernmost reached by the Caribs. The Spanish never settled them successfully. The Dutch tried and failed in the seventeenth century. It was Denmark that first successfully occupied these jewels of the sea, and Christian V took possession in 1671.

The three larger islands remained Danish until World War I. Then the United States, with a need

for Caribbean bases, bought them from the Danes. The smaller British Virgin Islands lie to the east of St. John. They have been English since 1672, and Tortola is the largest of the Virgins in the British colony. The U.S. Virgins, which include many small islands as well as the three larger ones, have the status of an organized but unincorporated territory and are under the jurisdiction of the U.S. Department of the Interior. Residents of the islands are U.S. citizens but do not vote in U.S. presidential elections. They elect their unicameral legislature.

U.S. VIRGIN ISLANDS

The three largest of the Virgin Islands were sold by Denmark to the United States for $25,000,000 in 1917. The U.S. Virgin Islands are an unincorporated territory with a governor elected by popular vote. The population is approximately 75,000. English is the principal language, but Spanish and French are also spoken. The scenery is outstandingly beautiful, especially in the National Park in St. John and the Reef National Monument at St. Croix. There are fine freeport stores, excellent hotels, good beaches, fishing and treasure diving and good airline connections to the U.S., Canada, other Caribbean islands and South America. The average annual temperature is 78° F. Of the approximately 1,300,000 visitors annually, 470,000 arrive on cruise ships.

ST. THOMAS

Bathed by the Atlantic Ocean on the north and washed by the Caribbean on the southern shore, St. Thomas is the second largest, most densely populated and most accessible Virgin of them all. Lively St. Thomas is an island of contrasts. Beside a great deep-water harbor rises the most attractive capital city, called Charlotte Amalie. This lively cosmopolitan city has more hundred-year-old buildings in use today than any other city its size in the United States. Here visitors enjoy Dutch doors, Danish roof lines, French grillwork, Spanish patios and modern U.S. resort hotels. Here dwelt Captain Kidd and Bluebeard. From this port Sir Francis Drake harried Spanish fleets. Today ships carrying tourists and provisioning the islands fill the harbor.

Charlotte Amalie, named for the consort of Christian V, rises via a series of terraced set-backs to the heights of three hills called Denmark, Synagogue and Government. Pastel-hued houses are strewn about like so many colored toys. Despite the ravages of time, hurricanes and modern improvements the city retains its aspect of an eighteenth century Caribbean port. Narrow cobbled streets, old walls, winding lanes, warehouses that are centuries old, stone stairways and old Danish names — *Kronprindsen Gade, Dronningens Gade* — are reminiscent of its colonial past.

If we set off on foot at the bottom of the city, the first outstanding sites to see are the magnificent old terra cotta warehouses that run from Main Street to the harbor. By removing layers of encrustation, the present occupant shop owners have uncovered soaring arches of magnificent brick and stone, floors laid with fine Italian tiles and Spanish marble. Thick walls and breezeways provide air-conditioning. The buildings are as attractive as the freeport imports they display: silver, china, perfume, liquor and silks. A shopping area is called Beretta Center, named for a St. Thomian of Italian descent who was among the first to uncover these rare architectural treasures. Camille Pissarro, the great Impressionist painter, was born in quarters nearby.

ST. THOMAS

ST. JOHN

SIR FRANCIS DRAKE CHANNEL

CARIBBEAN SEA

A landmark of the city is Old Fort Christian, built three hundred years ago. It has been used as a jail, church, courthouse and governor's residence.

The second oldest Jewish synagogue in the New World is on St. Thomas. The floor of the temple is covered with sand commemorating the biblical exodus of the Jews from Egypt over the scorching desert. Charming Government House, with a wrought-iron balcony stands near the top of the interesting Street of 99 steps. Hotel 1829 is named for the date of its construction and was once a splendid patrician town house. French Town or "Cha Cha Town" is a French village at the west end of the harbor, a fascinating enclave of descendants of Breton and Norman émigrés to the New World.

The vista from Skyline Drive at the top of Charlotte Amalie, overlooking the port and town, is unforgettable. The island of St. Thomas is cut in two by a mountain range. To the north of the mountains are panoramic views of the Atlantic, Magens Bay Beach, and the emerald-green British Virgin Islands lying in the distance. Tours of the island reveal numerous other points of interest.

Hosting the tidal wave of tourists that has inundated the island are a wide variety of beach-front and hilltop hotels ranging from the luxurious to modest guest houses. Shopping is a prime pleasure, for prices of the most exquisite imported merchandise are low enough to inspire a gleam in the eye of the most cautious shopper. Fishing, swimming and all sorts of water sports draw visitors back to the island again and again. St. Thomas is the lively, swinging Virgin, and the bongo beat throbs in many hotel nightclubs and in colorful native clubs in Charlotte Amalie.

ST. JOHN

St. John has thirty-one sandy bays, green mountains, bay tree forests, white sand beaches, blue waters, cool mountain streams and deep valleys. On the slopes of Bordeaux Mountain, 1,288 feet in height, grow wild orchids, bromeliads and many brightly blooming trees and vines.

This is the smallest of the three major U.S. Virgins, but is almost the same size as St. Thomas, twenty-one square miles as compared with twenty-seven. St. John lies three miles east of St. Thomas across Pillsbury Sound. It has a climate so favorable that it is said that the common cold does not exist there.

St. John was settled in 1716, the second island to be taken over by the Danes, after St. Thomas. By 1731 there were 109 estates cultivating the very fertile soil. St. John's Coral Bay was judged by no less an authority than Admiral Nelson to have the best harbor in the Lesser Antilles. Larger than that of Charlotte

Amalie, Coral Bay could accommodate two hundred to three hundred ships at a time. The economic outlook of St. John was indeed promising.

Then in 1733 the slaves of St. John revolted, killing almost all whites, burning and pillaging. The magnificent stone ruins at Annaberg plantation were the site of the end of the revolt. There, surrounded by French troops, the black men shot one another and the women and children threw themselves into the sea.

Ever since then the island has been quiet and comparatively undeveloped. Natives, easy-going and relaxed, collect leaves from bay trees for the rum factory on St. Thomas, make charcoal, weave fine baskets, and fish. The native families own much of the land and often refuse to part with any of it, regardless of price. They have for generations been so deeply attached to their own plot of soil that even the most lucrative offers have been met with indifference.

However, Laurance Rockefeller was able to buy five thousand of the island's most scenic acres, which he gave to the U.S. Government to form the Virgin Islands National Park, now covering two-thirds of the island. He also purchased Caneel Bay Plantation and there built an elegant modern resort, complete with golf course, spacious lawns and broad beaches. Other new hotels have been built and there are some guest houses and cottage colonies, plus camping facilities within the National Park at Cinnamon Bay.

Point of entry to the island by boat is Cruz Bay, and here there is a tiny village of the same name, the main settlement of St. John.

On St. John one can still wander through old orchards and discover huge sugar cauldrons filled with bright flowers. Petroglyphs of pre-Columbian days abound. Old muskets, iron chests, cannon and other relics of St. John's past are frequently found. A ten-mile center road and trail lead to the green hills.

ST. CROIX

St. Croix is the more quiet, once agricultural Virgin. Largest of the islands, it is twenty-eight miles long and ten miles wide. Almost all the land was under intensive cultivation, primarily in cattle raising and sugar cane production. In the great days of the plantations there were more than three hundred mansions, and many of them are still occupied. The island is known as "The Garden of the Antilles." Seven flags have floated over its quaint towns. These were the flags of Spain, Holland, France, the Knights of Malta, England, Denmark and the United States.

No flags flew over the Carib Indian villages, but there are more than forty Indian village sites. Archaeologists have found fascinating artifacts and stone slabs with petroglyphs and pictographs at Salt River. The Indians called the island "Ay, Ay" and Columbus named it Santa Cruz, which became St. Croix.

Christiansted, the tiny capital, is one of the most charming towns in the West Indies, an eighteenth century jewel. It has a beautifully preserved Old Danish port area, red-roofed eighteenth century pastel buildings in pink, blue and yellow, and everywhere a blaze of bougainvillea, hibiscus and other blooms. Shops are enclosed beneath cool, breezy arcades that contribute to the shoppers' pleasure. It's a lively and swinging town with good hotels, restaurants and night clubs.

The waterfront and town square of Christiansted is now a National Historic Site. Here is ancient Fort Christianvaern, built in 1743, complete with dungeons. It is the best preserved of the five forts still standing in the Virgin Islands. In Government House are fine replicas of original Danish furnishings. The first Lutheran Church in the islands, the Steeple Building, was built in 1753 and has been a hospital, a military bakery and a school. Across from Government House is the hardware store where Alexander Hamilton worked as a clerk at the age of eleven. The quaint alleys have fine freeport shops like those of Charlotte Amalie. In front of the harbor is Protestant

Cay, a colorful little island with one hotel, a beautiful beach and many sailboats for rent.

The other tiny town of the island, Frederiksted, is also quite picturesque. Rebuilt after a fire in 1878 along Victorian lines, its architecture is a quaint melange of Colonial Danish and all the baroque curlicues, cupolas and gazebos that were the rage during Victoria's era. The small old fort, Frederiksfort, built in 1671, was the site of the proclamation abolishing slavery in the Virgin Islands. It now serves as a police station and museum.

Several of the gracious old estate houses on the island are open to the public. Along the way to these, the visitor will see picturesque ruins of old plantations, witnesses to the fact that Cruzian slaves did not take kindly to bondage. Time and again slave rebellions broke out, only to be crushed with great loss of life and property.

The graceful names of these estates are evocative: Anna's Hope, Good Hope, Upper Love, Lower Love, Jealousy, Sally's Fancy. One of the plantations, called Judith's Fancy, is modeled after a French palace and was once the residence of the Governor of the Knights of Malta. Whim Greathouse, which was built in 1794, has been restored by the St. Croix Landmarks Society.

Scores of resorts, inns, hotels and guest houses have been built in recent years to accommodate the ever-increasing number of visitors coming to the island to fish, enjoy the water world, and relax. A jet airport accommodates direct flights from the U.S. mainland.

THE BRITISH VIRGIN ISLANDS

These beautiful, quiet islands with forest covered mountains rising to 1,500 feet above sea level are surrounded by deep, blue, clear water. They contain sixty islands and cays, cover 69 square miles, and only seventeen are inhabited. The government is ministerial, with general elections. Road Town on Tortola is the capital. Of approximately 12,500 inhabitants, 10,000 live on Tortola, 1,500 on Virgin Gorda. There are numerous good but mostly small resorts, hotels and guesthouses. The largest is Little Dix Bay Hotel on Virgin Gorda. The airport on Beef Island has airline connections with St. Thomas, Puerto Rico and other Caribbean Islands. The British Virgins play host to approximately 65,000 visitors annually, and the language is English.

Not counting all the little cays, there are about 40 British Virgins, of which only 17 are inhabited. Tortola is the largest with about 10,000 inhabitants, next is Virgin Gorda with approximately 1,500 people. The islands are mountainous, highest is Sage Mountain (1780 ft.) on Tortola with a beautiful rain forest.

Tranquil is the word for these islands. They embody many Americans' (especially northerners')

British Virgin Islands

dream of a serene, remote South Sea island, the dream of a perfect vacation. There are 30 hotels, inns and guest houses with about 1000 beds, the year 'round temperature is between 77°-85°, at night 10-15° less, no really rainy season, last hurricane in 1924. There are about 120 boats for charter with additional 500 beds.

And what great sports and recreation: Unexcelled sailing, fishing (four world records include an 845 lb. Marlin), diving (beautiful coral reefs and plenty of ancient shipwrecks), swimming and tennis. No golf, no TV, no bigtime entertainment, no noisy jetport. There is spectacular sightseeing, sunning on quiet, isolated white beaches, dancing at the hotels, one movie theater and shopping in Road Town, Tortola, capital of the islands. There is a hospital with 9 doctors and plenty of churches: Catholic, Anglican, Baptist, Methodist, Seventh Day Adventist, Church of God, Jehovahs Witnesses and Pentecostal.

The islands are about 60 miles east of Puerto Rico, 12 miles east of St. Thomas, U.S. Virgin Islands, with excellent flight connections from both.

The total population is a little more than 12,000, under British rule for over 300 years. Currency is the U.S. Dollar.

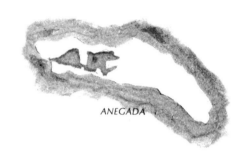

ANEGADA

GUANA ISLAND
GREAT CAMANOE
VIRGIN GORDA
JOST VAN DYKE
BEEF ISLAND
TORTOLA
GINGER ISLAND
COOPER ISLAND
PETER ISLAND
CARIBBEAN SEA
NORMAN ISLAND

N
S

ST. MAARTEN

This partly Dutch and partly French island contains thirty-seven square miles of land and a population of approximately 12,500 souls. Friendly mountain scenery, good beaches, excellent hotels, complete freeport, fine gift shops and excellent fishing attract visitors. Philipsburg is the Dutch capital, Marigot the French. There are good airline connections to other Caribbean islands and the United States. English, Dutch and French are spoken. Of the 185,000 visitors annually, about 60,000 come aboard cruise ships.

The visitor to St. Maarten can enjoy two different worlds, and both are delightful. This charming speck of land in the arc of islands that form the Lesser Antilles covers thirty-seven square miles. Of these, sixteen square miles are Dutch and twenty-one are French. The Dutch call their portion of the island Sint Maarten. The French portion is Saint Martin. The people speak English and live in good neighborly fashion without friction. Dutch St. Maarten is a member of the Netherlands Antilles, and Philipsburg is the principal town. French St. Martin is a commune of the department of Guadeloupe, one of France's four overseas departments. Marigot is its principal town. There is no problem going back and forth across the borders of the two sections of this peaceful island.

Columbus gave the island its name in 1493 when he sailed past on his second voyage on November 11, saint's day of St. Martin de Tours. Caribs lived there, and early settlers avoided them. St. Maarten became a harbor of refuge for Dutch vessels in 1620, and the Dutch built a fort. They found salt beds and began the export of salt, an important trade item. The French in 1629 built a small fort on the island. The Spanish reconquered St. Martin in 1633 and built another fort on the heights above Point Blanch.

Peter Stuyvesant, who was later to become the first governor of New Amsterdam, lost his leg here while leading a Dutch attack on the Spaniards in 1644. The Dutch and French returned in 1648 and made a treaty of friendship.

During the next two centuries the flags flying over the island changed sixteen times, and English fleets were continually attacking. Since 1816 the Dutch have had control over their portion of the island.

English became the prevailing language of both the Dutch and French sections by the middle of the eighteenth century. Nearby St. Eustatius was an important port supplying arms and ammunition to the American revolutionaries during the infancy of the United States.

Cattle, sugar cane, cotton and sisal were the principal products of the island in the nineteenth century. In the first decades of the twentieth century many of the natives of St. Maarten left home to work in the oil refineries of Curaçao and Aruba.

Today St. Maarten, as a member of the six islands of the Netherlands Antilles, is an equal partner in the Kingdom of the Netherlands. There is universal suffrage. The executive of the Netherlands Windward Islands is the Lieutenant Governor, appointed by the Queen of the Netherlands. In the French portion of the island the mayor, who is elected by voters, administers St. Martin and St. Barthélemy.

Roads, airports and radio-telephone communications were built in the 1960s with a grant from the Netherlands Government. A drive to court tourists was launched at that time. Tax advantages were designed to increase the building of hotels and new industries. There are no import duties and no excise taxes.

The island today offers numerous delightful and individual hotels, excellent facilities for cruise ships and visiting yachtsmen, splendid restaurants, great beaches with wonderful coral reefs in the surrounding waters, and gambling in continental casinos. More and more visitors are learning that life can be sweet in St. Maarten, and the people are prospering and happy.

The map shows the island of St. Eustatius with the following labels: VENUS BAAI, JENKINS BAY, St., BARGINE BAY, GOLDEN ROCK AIRPORT, COMPAGNIE BAAI, FORT ROYAL, ROUND HILL, ORANJESTAD, THE QUILL, GALLOWS BAY, Eustatius, KAY BAY, BUCCANEER'S BAY, N

ST. EUSTATIUS

The lonely volcanic island, the Golden Rock, rises from the depths southeast of Puerto Rico. Part of the Netherlands Antilles, the island prospered in the seventeenth and eighteenth centuries until the settlements were destroyed by the British in 1781 for assistance to and recognition of the American revolutionaries. The island boasts one hotel and two guesthouses. English and Dutch are spoken.

Spell it Sint Eustatius and call it Statia. It is a lonely little island, an arid plain between two low mountains. The Quill, 1,800 feet above sea level, is the highest elevation. Today there are about 2,000 inhabitants, many of Indian descent. During the American Revolution 20,000 people lived there and often as many as two hundred sailing ships loaded with arms, ammunition and supplies for the revolutionaries were anchored in the port at Oranjestad. In those days Statia was The Golden Rock.

The visitors who reach this backwater in time may not know or remember that once St. Eustatius was a key port of the Caribbean and the principal base of the great Dutch sea-farers of the seventeenth and eighteenth centuries. Franklin D. Roosevelt knew and remembered, and on the island is a plaque sent by that U. S. president in 1939 in gratitude for the help Statia gave to the U.S.A. in winning the war against England. A British admiral in 1781 said, "This Rock, only six miles in length and three in width, has done England more harm than all the arms of her most potent enemies, and alone supported this infamous rebellion."

Statia's stormy past is in great contrast to its quiet life today. Only one of the fine old mansions of the great Dutch traders remains. Almost all of the people are black, and they work hard at farming and raising goats, sheep and cattle. The little island is Dutch, one of the Netherlands Antilles, but everybody speaks English. It is in truth a rock, infertile. There are two guest houses, a new hotel on the beach, and several steel bands. Statia is fifteen minutes from St. Maarten by air.

SABA

A landmark of the Caribbean, Saba is a beachless cone, the top of an extinct volcano, with 2,900-foot Mt. Scenery its highest point. It contains five square rocky miles and a population of 1,000 that speaks English and Dutch. The capital is Bottom. The average annual temperature is 80° F. There is an airline connection with St. Maarten and several good guest-houses offer pleasant hospitality.

Unique, unforgettable Saba is an extinct volcano rising out of the sea on the edge of the Atlantic in the Lesser Antilles. It has no beaches, no fringing coral reefs. Cloud-wreathed Mount Scenery is the highest peak, 2,900 feet above sea level. It is the smallest of the three windward islands of the Netherlands Antilles. Saba lies twenty-eight miles south of St. Maarten and seventeen miles northeast of St. Eustatius.

Columbus sighted Saba in 1493, as he sailed toward Cuba. It has changed flags twelve times, bouncing back and forth among the Dutch, French, Spanish and English. Though the Dutch first settled here, Saba has always been English-speaking. For centuries the men of Saba have gone to sea, and today still have reputation as excellent sailors.

The four charming and colorful villages on Saba are Hell's Gate, Windwardside, St. John and The Bottom. The Bottom is the principal village. The name is derived from the Dutch word "botte," which means bowl. The tiny villages of Hell's Gate and Windwardside are perched on the crest of the volcano, and these villages near the top of the mountain are cool and wind-washed. All are quaint, snug places with a Dutch flavor, lushly blooming tropical trees and flowers. There is a hospital, schools, and in each village a small library. The neat cottages have red-shingled roofs, white picket fences and green shutters. The atmo-sphere is idyllic, peaceful, evocative of a colorful past.

Daily flights from St. Maarten swoop in over the rim of the crater to land on the airstrip. Arriving by sea is even more of an adventure than arriving by air. Ships must anchor in either Fort Bay or Ladder Bay, and passengers are taken to shore in small boats. The road up the steep cliff is winding and narrow, and there are only six miles of road on the little island. The villages have several nice, old-fashioned guest houses, with good, simple food.

The population of Saba is about one thousand people, half of them white and half of them black. There were never many slaves on the island, for there is so little land to cultivate. Many of the men of Saba still go to sea, or to work in the oil refineries in Curaçao and Aruba. Some Sabans farm, build boats, and raise goats and cows. The exquisite embroidery of the Saban women, called Spanish work, has long been famous throughout the Caribbean.

The land is green, the air is cool, and mountain climbing up Booby Hill and to Mount Scenery's crater is exhilarating. There are beautiful views from the heights of this small world cupped in a bowl of rock. Hours can be spent most pleasantly strolling down narrow lanes and savoring the unique flavor of life on Saba.

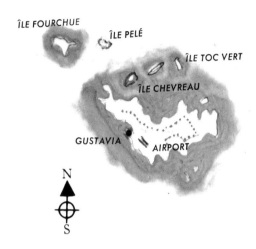

ÎLE FOURCHUE
ÎLE PELÉ
ÎLE TOC VERT
ÎLE CHEVREAU
GUSTAVIA
AIRPORT

N
S

ST. BARTHELEMY

This is a French island, a dependency of Guadeloupe, covering twenty-five square miles that support a population of 2,450. It has an excellent safe harbor, fine accommodations, freeport shopping, an interesting history and air connections with St. Maarten and Guadeloupe. The languages are French and English.

They call it St. Barts, and it is a refreshing hideaway in the uppermost corner of the Lesser Antilles, fifteen miles southeast of St. Maarten. Although the island was first settled by the French and is French today, it was a Swedish colony from 1784 to 1877. The only town on the island is Gustavia, named for a Swedish king.

Volcanic rocks cover the hillsides of the eight square miles of land. Coral reefs and shallows surround the island. There are some magnificent beaches on the north shore. Lobster fishing in the clear waters brings in a considerable income to the islanders. The people are friendly, frugal and orderly, hospitable to strangers. Most of the natives speak English and French. Many of the men go to sea while the women stay home and weave straw. There are a number of attractive sea-side resorts,

and the delectable food is French with Caribbean overtones. There is none of the glitter of the larger islands luring tourists, no nightclubs, not even a local radio station.

This peaceful bit of rocky, beach-fringed land is a hideaway for several internationally-known millionaires. Here David Rockefeller has a magnificent vacation home. The Moore family of Moore-McCormack Lines owns land, as does Edmond Rothschild. Though the island is off the beaten path, it is an excellent free-port shopping center for perfumes, crystal, handmade embroideries, microscopes, cameras, Dutch pewter, fine sweaters, liquors and wine. Sailing trips to nearby islands can be combined with excellent fishing for dolphin, marlin, wahoo, albacore and amberjack. Boats and guides are available.

ST. CHRISTOPHER (ST. KITTS)

England's first colony in the Caribbean, St. Kitts, is a volcanic island with a fascinating past and impressive historical monuments. Today it is a "state in voluntary association with Great Britain." The parliamentary government, with an elected House of Assembly and a Premier with Cabinet as executive branch, unites St. Christopher, Nevis and Anguilla as one state. Their combined population is approximately 57,000. St. Kitts comprises sixty-five square miles. Principal income of the three islands is from sugar and sea island cotton. There are many good small hotels and guesthouses and visitors number approximately 18,000 annually. Flight connections to other Caribbean islands, the U.S. and Canada are good. English is the language.

St. Christopher has been called St. Kitts since 1623, when the English arrived and settled this island in the northerly leeward group of the Lesser Antilles. It was their first colony in the Caribbean, and became known to the English as the "Mother Colony of the West Indies." Vast fertile plains spread around a volcanic peak. The Carib Indians called St. Kitts Liaguiga, "the fertile land." Mount Misery is the cloud-capped peak of the central mountain range and rises 4,314 feet. Sugar cane is the principal crop of St. Kitts. Cotton and vegetables are grown on the lower slopes of the mountains. Higher up are lush green forests. The black-sand beaches are of volcanic origin, as are those of many of the neighboring islands.

The French settled on a portion of St. Kitts in 1627, and struggled with the English for possession for almost a century. England has had full title to the island since 1783. The French left the capital, Basseterre. The port of Basseterre is at crossroads of the Leeward Islands, and here schooners from nearby Antigua, St. Maarten and Montserrat anchor alongside freighters from England, the United States and Canada.

The most impressive man-made artifact on the island is the massive fortress, Brimstone Hill, built by the British in the eighteenth century. It is a monumental structure, and the view from the top of the 750-foot fort is spectacular, with the horizon rimmed with peaks of neighboring islands. A winding road on which a car can be driven reaches almost to the top.

St. Kitts was once home to a man who gave his name to the flaming poinciana tree that has become one of the most colorful glories of the Caribbean. He was Phillipe de Longvilliers de Poincy, who ruled the island during twenty-one years of French possession. The remains of the Chateau of

M. de Poincy may be seen by making arrangements with the Fountain Estate House.

Tourism is in its infancy on St. Kitts. Expeditions around the countryside can be fascinating. Mount Misery entices mountain climbers. Part of the way to the peak is through scenic flatlands, but then it is a challenging climb to the crater of the extinct volcano. Agile mountaineers can enjoy a descent into the crater. In another extinct volcano on the ridge is a lake, Bos D'Ane Pond. The best areas for swimming are at Conaree Beach, Frigate Bay, Friar's Bay and the beaches around the Salt Ponds on the southern tip of the island. Here several salt crops are harvested each year. There is a modern hotel on Cockleshell Bay. In Basseterre there is a waterfront hotel. The sights of the busy waterfront, which is also the marketplace, are fascinating.

NEVIS

Southeast of St. Kitts lies Nevis, a thirty-six square mile island with 13,200 inhabitants. Alexander Hamilton was born here, Admiral Nelson stationed here. The scenery is attractive, the beaches splendid and the highest point is Nevis Peak, 3,596 feet. The island has several good small hotels, cottage colonies, guesthouses, and daily airplane and motor launch connections with St. Kitts. It is linked in statehood with St. Kitts and Anguilla. Everybody speaks English.

This leisurely, tranquil and beautiful little island was named Nuestra Senora de la Nieves, "Our Lady of the Snows," by Columbus because its mountain, Nevis Peak, is almost always wrapped in white clouds. The small island is eight miles long, six miles wide, and its slopes are covered with greenery, flowers and fruit trees. It is linked to its neighbors in the Leeward Antilles by air service from Antigua and a ferry from St. Kitts. Pinney Beach is a long, golden strand shaded by coconut palms.

In the days of the great sugar plantations, Nevis was of some importance. Captain John Smith stopped here for supplies and he and his crew enjoyed bathing in the warm mineral pools. Alexander Hamilton was born on Nevis. A young British Captain, Horatio Nelson, was married here to an attractive widow, Frances Nisbet, and a future king of England, Prince Clarence, was his best man. The record of the marriage is in St. John's Church at Fig Tree Village.

Today the majority of the people are black, and they are gracious and hospitable to strangers. Charlestown, the chief village, is small. The first capital, Jamestown, slid into the sea in an earthquake in 1680. There are a few new hotels, an attractive inn perched on a cliff, and other hostelries that were once great plantation homes. Some of the native dishes are a gourmet's delight— pixilated pork, turtle steak, egg plant soup and the roe of sea urchins.

ANGUILLA

Anguilla, near St. Maarten, is a flat island noted for salt production, good fishing and a plastic factory. It covers thirty-five square miles and the language is English. There are several small hotels, beach cottages and guest houses. With St. Kitts and Nevis it is a state associated with Great Britain.

St. Maarten, twelve miles across the Anguilla channel, is the nearest neighbor to Anguilla. Anguilla means, "eel" in Spanish and, indeed, the island does have a serpentine shape. It is a low land with fine beaches, sixteen miles long and two miles wide. It has been called the forgotten island.

After the wars of the colonial empires in the West Indies, Anguilla was in British hands, and English is the language today. The United States built an airstrip on the island in World War II. In 1967 St. Kitts, Nevis and Anguilla were granted commonwealth status and independence in their internal affairs by Great Britain. Friction erupted, and the Anguillians revolted against domination by St. Kitts, but there was no bloodshed.

Fishing is excellent in the surrounding waters, and the islanders are good boat-builders. Salt has been harvested at Sandy Ground for centuries. Most of the native islanders, however, work in Jamaica, St. Thomas, and other neighboring islands. Anguilla has yet to come out of the economic doldrums that held so many of the islands for ages, but the people, predominantly black, are nice to the few visitors who enjoy Anguilla's beautiful beaches.

ANTIGUA

Antigua, with its dependencies the islands of Barbuda and Redonda, is a state in association with the United Kingdom with full internal self-government. Splendid scenery, beautiful beaches, famous historical monuments, many first class hotels and resorts, golf, tennis, yachts for charter, deep sea fishing, hunting (deer, ducks and pigeons) are among its attractions to approximately 90,000 visitors annually. Of these, 30,000 arrive on cruise ships. The capital of this highly developed island is St. Johns, with a good deep water harbor. The average temperature is 80° F. A population of approximately 64,000 lives on the island's 108 square miles. They speak English. There are excellent airline connections with the U.S., Canada, Europe, South America and the other Caribbean islands.

Antigua was one of the first islands to be "discovered" by jet-set sun-seekers. This Leeward Island on the edge of the Atlantic has played host to many visitors including Queen Elizabeth and Princess Margaret. English Harbour is a favorite anchorage for cruising yachtsmen. Tourists enjoy all the amenities.

Antigua, with Barbuda and Redonda, has full internal self-government in association with Great Britain in independent statehood. The people are predominantly black, the language is English. Agricultural pursuits are on the wane; industry and tourism are on the rise. The 108 square miles of land are fringed by some of the finest beaches in the Caribbean. The soil is fertile, with fields and pastures and low rolling hills. The island is green with native forests and with imported flowering and fruit trees.

St. John's on the northwest coast, is the capital of Antigua. It has an excellent deep water har-

bor where cruise ships dock. The man-made harbor was completed in 1968 and can accommodate vessels drawing thirty-five feet. St. John's is a bustling port city, with many free-port shops, banks, cinemas and art galleries. St. John's cathedral, on top of the hill, is beautiful.

On the southern coast, English Harbour and Nelson's Dockyard are delightful attractions, the mecca of yachtsmen. From this base Lord Nelson, then Captain Nelson, sailed against England's foes in the Caribbean. In 1949 English Harbour was a ghost town, abandoned and decaying. In that year the Nicholson family sailed in there to refit, on their way to Australia. There they stayed, and chartered their fine yacht. That was the beginning of the renaissance of English Harbour, today one of the most popular ports for yachtsmen in those seas. The harbor is rimmed by old forts, and is a delightful place to explore.

Many of the people of Antigua work on farms,

others in the tourist hotels. Sugar cane is the most important crop. Sea Island cotton is also exported. Vegetables, fruit, beef cattle and poultry are raised, principally for local consumption. A large fishing fleet brings in excellent catches of fish and lobster.

The most important industry on the island is an oil refinery, the result of a twenty-five year agreement made between Standard Oil Company of Indiana and the government in 1961. The sugar cane becomes good rum for export. Concrete blocks, clothing, furniture, aluminum products, arrowroot starch, pottery and cotton seed meal and cake are some of the products manufactured on Antigua.

Visitors can find all they need to enjoy a perfect vacation. There are more than two dozen resort hotels. Everything is at hand for water sports—great beaches, excellent offshore fishing, a good charter fishing fleet, water-skiing, skin-diving, sunken ships to explore off Barbuda, and yachts for charter. Golf courses, tennis courts and duty-free shopping are also among the amusements.

BARBUDA

A dependency of Antigua, this flat island contains sixty-two square miles with beautiful beaches, excellent fishing and good hunting. Once a slave-breeding center of the Caribbean, it is historically interesting. There are air connections with Antigua. The language is English.

Barbuda makes an attractive target for a sailing expedition from Antigua. It lies twenty-five miles north of Antigua and is sixty-two square miles in area. Barbuda, once known as Dulcina, is a flat coral island with a large lagoon on the western side. It has miles and miles of pink and white sand beaches. The principal village is Codrington, and there is an attractive hotel there. A small air strip is nearby. The population is little more than a thousand, and most of the people make their living by fishing and catching lobster. Barbuda is a sportsman's paradise, for deer, wild pig, guinea fowl, pigeons and ducks are plentiful.

MONTSERRAT

This colorful green mountainous island with its hot sulphur springs lies near Antigua, and there are daily airline connections between the two islands. Chance Mountain at 3,000 feet is the highest point. It comprises thirty-nine square miles and has a population of 14,700. Plymouth, the capital, enjoys some attractive theatrical productions, golf, tennis, yachting, cricket and has several good small hotels. Approximately 10,000 visitors come to English-speaking Montserrat annually.

More American retirees have made their homes in Montserrat than in any of the other islands. It is an alluring and salubrious haven, and many attractive retirement homes have been built there. The mountainous cone of land is ribbed by deep green valleys with clear, flowing little mountain streams (called "guts"). There is a feeling of remoteness from hustle-bustle.

Once this was a land of fertile sugar and cotton plantations. When slaves were freed, most white people left. Many black islanders also departed to earn their living in the British Isles, for this was an English colony. Tomatoes, cotton and cattle are the principal crops today. With the influx of Canadians and Americans making their

Montserrat

N
S

HELL'S GATE

RENDEZVOUS BAY

ST. JOHNS VILLAGE

YELLOW HOLE

BUNKUM BAY

AIRPORT

ST. PETERS VILLAGE

SPANISH POINT

FARM BAY

CENTER HILLS

PLYMOUTH

SOUFRIÈRE HILLS

ST. PATRICK'S VILLAGE

SOUTH SOUFRIÈRE

GERMANS BAY

LANDING BAY

CARIBBEAN SEA

second homes here, there is a new lift in the economy.

The beaches are black volcanic sand, but enjoyable. The energetic explorer can hike up on the mountains through the rain forest and inspect a "soufriere," a hot volcanic sulphur spring. A popular pastime is hunting the giant mountain frog, the "crapaud," a delicacy known as mountain chicken.

There are several hotels in Plymouth, the principal town, and on the cliffs. Saturday is Plymouth's big day, when all the back-country people bring their produce to the town's "Green Market." The Montserrat Yacht Club offers facilities for yachtsmen, and sports include cricket, golf and tennis.

GUADELOUPE

An overseas department of France, Guadeloupe is a large double island (Basse-Terre and Grand-Terre) of 584 square miles and a population of 325,000. Basse-Terre has beautiful mountain scenery, Grand-Terre fertile flat land. The largest city is Pointe-a-Pitre, with a good harbor and excellent airline connections to North and South America, Europe and the other Caribbean islands. Visitors, at the rate of about 131,000 annually, enjoy first class hotels and resorts famous for outstanding cuisines, good auto roads, some of the best beaches in the West Indies, sailing, tennis, fishing, guided mountain climbing and cockfights. The natives speak French. Island dependencies of Guadeloupe are Marie Galante, Les Saintes, La Désirade, St. Barthelemy and St. Martin.

Guadeloupe rises from the sea in the arc of the Lesser Antilles, five hundred miles from Caracas, Venezuela, and 310 miles from Puerto Rico. It is really twin islands that resemble in shape the two wings of a butterfly. Together they cover an area of about 690 square miles. They are separated by a natural channel, the Rivière Salée (Salt River). A bridge spans the mangrove-fringed channel.

The western island, Basse-Terre, also called "Guadeloupe proprement dite," is a rugged and

Guadeloupe

hilly country. One of the Spanish discoverers of the island described it as "a large mountain which seemed to want to reach to heaven." One peak reaches 4,900 feet. Grande-Terre, the eastern of the twin islands, is flat and fertile. The languages spoken on Guadeloupe are French and a Creole dialect.

Columbus discovered this land on his second voyage. Carib Indians living there called the island "Karukera" (Island of Beautiful Waters). Beautiful indeed are the waterfalls that come from so high up that they seem to fall from out of the sky. The Caribs discouraged the Spanish attempts to colonize Guadeloupe for more than a hundred years, and the Spaniards gave up trying to settle there in 1604.

The French were the first to successfully settle the island in 1635, with L'Olive and DuPlessis as leaders. For more than two centuries the European powers fought over the beautiful island. The English made many attacks and gained control in the Seven Years War (1759-1766). After giving up Guadeloupe to the French, the English again cap-

Continued on page 84

63

Description of the following pictures

page 65

POINTE DES CHATEAUX, EAST END OF GUADELOUPE

One of the more spectacular views in the Caribbean is the east end of Guadeloupe (Grand-Terre), Pointe des Châteaux, with its picturesque rock formations. Great waves break against these dark rocks, and the clouds are driven swiftly by the steady trade winds. A good auto road leads from St. François to the point where this picture was taken.

page 66

GUADELOUPE: TERRE DE HAUT, LES SAINTES

Off the southeastern coast of Basse-Terre and facing the town of Trois Rivières is the island group Les Saintes, which can be reached by boat or plane from Guadeloupe. It is a group of five hilly islands with several villages and beautiful scenery. Terre de Haut and Terre de Bas are the important ones. The picture shows Terre de Haut, with residents of Breton and Norman descent who, with few exceptions, are fishermen. Just outside of Terre de Haut on Ilet à Cabrit is a first rate hotel, "Fort Josephine." It has a main house with bungalows and is a paradise for sports fishermen.

VIEW FROM GOSIER TO BASSE-TERRE, GUADELOUPE

A beautiful scene opens from Gosier over the ocean to Basse-Terre and its high mountains covered with dense tropical rain forests. Visible in the foreground is part of the fine beach around Gosier.

page 67

ROSEAU, CAPITAL OF DOMINICA

Surrounded by the high mountains of Dominica, Roseau is a town of about 15,000 inhabitants, still quite primitive, and with one good hotel, "Fort Young." The beauty of the island lies inland, in the high green mountains, the tropical vegetation, the streams and waterfalls, the plantations and the Carib Indian Reservation.

DOMINICA: CARIB INDIAN WOMAN

Deep in the mountains of Dominica but close to the coast is the Carib Indian Reservation, with about 1,500 inhabitants. It is governed by the Carib Council and a chief, who is now elected every three years. Their features are Asian and their skins reddish brown. They rarely mix with other races. Their main settlement, Salybia, has a school building and a Catholic church. Most of the Indians are Catholics.

page 68

HISTORICAL DIAMOND ROCK, MARTINIQUE

One of the great historical landmarks of the Caribbean, Diamond Rock, figured in the time of Napoleon I and the war between France and England. In 1804, the British occupied the rock with 110 sailors and one lieutenant. The French fleet became quite annoyed with the rock over the next seventeen months, but finally amid almost insurmountable difficulties the French stormed and captured it.

page 68

FORT-DE-FRANCE, CAPITAL OF MARTINIQUE

Superbly located on an excellent harbor, the capital is surrounded by hills and faces a wide bay beside the Caribbean Sea. This air view was taken on an incoming flight from the north to the nearby international airport, just a few miles to the south.

Continued on page 81

POINTE DES CHATEAUX, EAST END OF GUADELOUPE

*TERRE DE HAUT
LES SAINTES*

GUADELOUPE

For detailed description see page 64

*VIEW FROM
GOSIER TO
BASSE-TERRE*

ROSEAU, CAPITAL OF DOMINICA

DOMINICA

CARIB INDIAN WOMAN

67

HISTORICAL DIAMOND ROCK

MARTINIQUE

*FORT-DE-FRANCE,
CAPITAL OF MARTINIQUE*

SOUTH COAST WITH MT. LARCHER

MARTINIQUE

ST. PIERRE WITH MT. PELÉ

69

CASTRIES AND HARBOR

ST. LUCIA

For detailed description see page 81

←

THE PITONS
LANDMARKS OF
THE CARIBBEAN

PIGEON ISLAND FROM REDUIT BEACH

CARIBBEAN COAST, BARBADOS

CODRINGTON COLLEGE

BARBADOS

COUNTRYSIDE

HISTORICAL CAREENAGE

BARBADOS

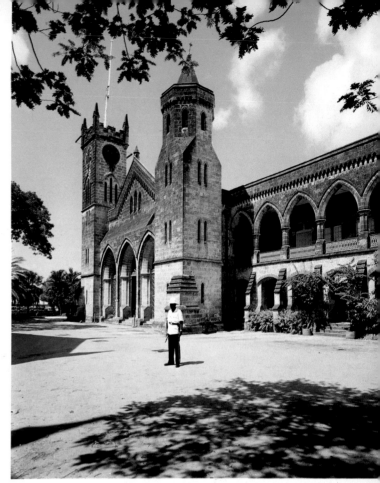

PUBLIC BUILDINGS, BRIDGETOWN

PEASANT HOME

For detailed description
see page 82

73

TOBAGO, AN EXOTIC ISLAND

STRIPED PORK FISH
AND CORAL

COLORFUL FISH, SPONGES, CORAL AND GORGONIANS

IN THE CLEAR
WARM WATERS
OF THE
CARIBBEAN SEA

CARNIVAL

TRINIDAD

For detailed description see page 82

STEEL BAND AND
LIMBO DANCERS

EAST INDIANS IN TRINIDAD

TRINIDAD

MOSQUE IN ST. JOSEPH

OLDEST BOTANICAL GARDEN
IN THE NEW WORLD

ST. VINCENT

BANANA LOADING

ST. VINCENT: DEEP WATER HARBOR OF KINGSTOWN

CARRIACOU

OVER THE
GRENADINES

PALM ISLAND

*Description of foregoing pictures -
continued from page 64*

page 69
MARTINIQUE: SOUTH COAST WITH MT. LARCHER

The southwest end of Martinique is dominated by Mt. Larcher. The picture was taken near Diamant, looking west along the southern coast.

page 69
MARTINIQUE: ST. PIERRE WITH MOUNT PELÉ

Along the entire western coast from the town of Schoelcher to the town of St. Pierre there are excellent beaches with fine grayish sand, a permanent reminder of the volcanic activity of Mount Pelé, which broods in the background. In 1902 St. Pierre was a lovely city of more than 30,000 inhabitants when it was totally destroyed by an eruption of Mount Pelé. Today the ruins tell the story not only of a fantastic disaster but also the great past of a town once called "Pearl of the Caribbean."

page 70
ST. LUCIA: THE PITONS

The two picturesque mountain peaks behind the schooner are the Pitons—Gros Piton and Petit Piton—rising sharply from the Caribbean Sea to heights of 2,619 feet and 2,461 feet respectively. Clearly outlined against the sky, they are outstanding landmarks of the Caribbean islands.

page 71
ST. LUCIA: CASTRIES AND HARBOR

Flanked by two hills, Castries, the capital of St. Lucia, has one of the loveliest and safest harbors and best yacht anchorages in the Caribbean. It is a favorite port of call for cruise ships. Only a few minutes from town is beautiful Vigie Beach, with a strand of white sand that stretches for more than three miles.

ST. LUCIA: PIGEON ISLAND FROM REDUIT BEACH

Reduit Beach on the northwest coast of St. Lucia is one of the best beaches of St. Lucia. Two elegant resorts are located there. In the background is Pigeon Island, connected by a causeway with the main island.

page 72
BARBADOS: CARIBBEAN COAST

The beautiful beaches in St. James Parish along the Caribbean Sea are called the Platinum Coast of Barbados. Some of the best resorts of Barbados are in this neighborhood: Sandy Lane, Coral Reef, Miramar, Colony Club and others. Sailing, fishing, water skiing, diving, snorkeling and boating are some of the many sports offered to the tourist here.

CODRINGTON COLLEGE

Christopher Codrington, founder of this seminary, was born in Barbados in 1668. In 1700 he became governor of the Leeward Islands, retiring to Barbados in 1707, where he died on Good Friday, April 7, 1710. He left his two sugar estates to the Society for the Propagation of the Gospel in London, to be used for the founding of a college for the study of religion and medicine, under vows of chastity, poverty and obedience on the lines of a monastic order. Anglican priests of the Community of the Resurrection in Mirfield (Yorkshire) keep up this work in affiliation with the University of Durham (England).

page 72
BARBADOS: COUNTRYSIDE

Hills with sugar cane fields and bananas, ancient greathouses of estates, sugar mill ruins, churches with old grave yards, palms, frangipani and casuarina trees—that's the countryside of Barbados. George Washington loved it. He wrote that he was "perfectly enraptured with the beautiful prospects . . . on every side the fields of cane, corn, fruit trees in a delightful green setting."

BARBADOS: HISTORICAL CAREENAGE
One of the landmarks of Barbados is this colorful inlet at Bridgetown, capital of the island. There are busy wharves where, for more than 300 years, ships of all makes and origins have docked for overhauling, cleaning and caulking. The scene is changing fast, old buildings are being replaced with new and modern ones, and in a few years it will all be very different. This is one of the most picturesque points in Barbados.

BARBADOS: PUBLIC BUILDINGS, BRIGETOWN
Built in 1874, these neo-gothic public buildings with an attractive inner court contain fine stained glass windows imported from England. Inside are chambers of the Senate and House of Assembly, and also the post office.

BARBADOS: PEASANT HOME
One of the most attractive features of Barbados is its cleanliness. Streets, buildings and even the homes of the peasantry are kept clean and tidy. Simply constructed—often with only a sheet of corrugated metal as a roof—these homes are kept shipshape and are beautified with flowerbeds.

TOBAGO, AN EXOTIC ISLAND
Can you imagine Robinson Crusoe in these surroundings? Tobagonians believe that Daniel Defoe had their romantic tropical island in mind when he created his masterpiece. Here are many small, sandy beaches set in coves or half-moon bays. The visitor succumbs easily to Tobago's sun-drenched attractions, the outstanding tropical vegetation, and particularly the exotic birds living here.

IN THE CLEAR, WARM WATERS OF THE CARIBBEAN SEA
A wonderland of exotic life, brilliant colors and unusual forms is revealed to the diver and snorkeler around the Caribbean islands. Colorful fish, coral, gorgonians, sponges and molluscs live in the reef formations surrounding most of the islands. Some are well known, such as the Buccoo Reef at Tobago, the Buck Island Reef National Monument at St. Croix, the Sea Gardens at Barbados and the reefs surrounding Grand Cayman. But there are so many more. One of the finest sea gardens at Tobago lies just outside of Arnos Vale on the northwestern coast of Tobago. Beautiful formations are around Antigua, and the reefs about the Grenadines are outstanding for their variety of sea life.

TRINIDAD: CARNIVAL
In all the world there is no carnival celebration to equal Trinidad's annual madness. Fantastic costumes, individual or worn by stylized groups, wild, noisy or harmonious music—these mark a spontaneous celebration climaxed with organized parades and shows on the Savannah and in Independence Square in Port-of-Spain. During this two-day delirium of sight and sound (Monday and Tuesday before Ash Wednesday) the streets of Port-of-Spain are overflowing with jubilant people jumping and stamping to the tunes and rhythms of steel bands and calypso groups. Our picture shows a typical street scene, alive with the carnival atmosphere.

TRINIDAD: STEEL BAND AND LIMBO DANCERS
The Caribbean's popularity all over the world during the last two decades must be credited in part to calypso, the steel band and the limbo, a form of dance which developed from an old African ritual of manhood. All three evolved and became formalized in Trinidad, and today can be heard and seen all over the West Indies and in the night-clubs of the United States, Canada and Europe. Oil drums are the major instrument of a typical steel band, while the limbo dancer attempts to "clear" under a bamboo bar as low as ten inches from the ground.

page 77
TRINIDAD: EAST INDIANS IN TRINIDAD
More than 300,000 East Indians comprise a large part of Trinidad's total population. These people, particularly the older ones, adhere strictly to their own customs and religion, colorfully expressed in their traditional garments, foods and in many small homes which are scattered all over Trinidad.

TRINIDAD: MOSQUE IN ST. JOSEPH
This is one of the many attractive mosques for the Muslim population of Trinidad. There are approximately 50,000 followers of the teachings of the Prophet Mohammed on the island.

page 78
ST. VINCENT: OLDEST BOTANICAL GARDEN IN THE NEW WORLD
More than 200 years old, this garden has a fine selection of tropical trees, including descendants of the original breadfruit seedlings brought to St. Vincent by Captain Bligh from Tahiti on his post-Bounty voyage in the Providence.

ST. VINCENT: BANANA LOADING
It is a colorful picture in the harbor, when the peasant women bring the harvest of their banana fields, well packed and carried on their heads, to the banana boat.

page 79
ST. VINCENT: DEEP WATER HARBOR OF KINGSTOWN
The modern deep water harbor of Kingstown invites many cruise ships to St. Vincent. It was also important to improve the harbor a few years ago because of the export of the island's agricultural produce. Agriculture is the basis of St. Vincent's economy and provides more than two-thirds of the total employment. The principal products are bananas, arrowroot, nutmeg, yams, coconut, cassava and sea island cotton. Kingstown is an impressive city, with its colorful gardens, stately churches, government buildings and attractive harbor.

page 80
OVER THE GRENADINES
About 125 peaks of an underwater mountain range rising out of the sea between St. Vincent and Grenada—these are the Grenadines. They range greatly in size and topography. Around the islands are large coral reef formations, which are visible in these views of Carriacou and Palm Island. Carriacou is one of the biggest of these islands. It has an airstrip like Palm Island with flight connections from Grenada, St. Lucia and St. Vincent. Fishing, diving and sailing is great in the Grenadines: quite a few sailboats are visible in the photograph of Palm Island.

Continued from page 63

tured the island in 1794, were driven out, held it again, and then discontinued the fighting. Since 1816 France has held Guadeloupe. Today it is an incorporated department of the Republic of France and its people have equal rights with the citizens of France.

Point-à-Pitre is the chief port and flourishing commercial center of Guadeloupe. It lies at the southern end of the Rivière Salée on Grande-Terre and gives an impression of a miniature, tropical Paris. On the other end of the mountainous island is Basse-Terre, the attractive capital city. Banana boats on the long pier, a seventeenth century cathedral, handsome residences and a huge old fortress, St. Charles, are among the interesting aspects of the capital.

From Basse-Terre a fine auto road leads along the coast, with unspoiled scenery and beautiful beaches. Arrangements can be made in that city for cars and guides for a fascinating excursion to the top of a dormant volcano, Sufrière. The road leads through a magnificent rain forest and the refreshing waters of natural hot springs are found along the roadside. Another enjoyable drive on Guadeloupe is the trip over the mountain on a new auto road, La Traversée. It leads through wild jungles and dense rain forests. Many charming and interesting villages and beautiful beaches are found throughout the twin islands. A stirring view that enchants artists and photographers is the sight of the surf breaking on huge rocks at Pointe des Chateaux on the southeast point of the island.

The people of Guadeloupe are warm and friendly. The girls of the island are famous throughout the Caribbean for their beauty and for their attractive costumes and elegant headdresses. The taxis waiting at the airport travel over comfortably passable roads. Good hotels and epicurean restaurants serve memorable food.

Guadeloupe has a group of nearby island dependencies and one, St. Barthélemy, lies one hundred miles to the north. Marie-Galante, a few miles southeast, covers sixty-one square miles. To the east is Desirade, beautiful and pastoral. Five little islands, Les Iles des Saintes, are just south of Guadeloupe.

LES SAINTES

This hilly island group close to the south end of Guadeloupe is remembered for a famous sea battle between the French and the British in 1782. It is linked to Guadeloupe with daily airplane and ferry service.

Small, green and hilly are Les Saintes, Guadeloupe's five little neighbors. Terre de Bas and Terre de Haut are the principal islands, linked to Guadeloupe by ferry and airplane. Though they are idyllically remote, there is an excellent new hotel at Ilet à Cabrit just outside Terre de Haut. This is a sports fisherman's heaven.

The natives of the islands are intriguing. Most of the population of Terre de Bas is black. The majority of residents of Terre de Haut are white, descended from sea-faring Bretons and Normans who settled there long ago. Many still make their living today by fishing.

The men wear quaint hats, unique among the islands. It is woven of straw and bamboo, shaped like a parasol and is about a foot and a half in diameter. It is covered with a white fabric and attached to the top of a cylinder that fits tightly on the head. The hat, called a "salaco," resembles those worn by Chinese coolies.

DOMINICA

A pristine mountain island with many rivers and beautiful tropical vegetation contains 290 square miles with a population of 71,000 who speak English and French. Here there is a Carib Indian reservation. The capital, Roseau, has an interesting botanical garden. Approximately 18,500 visitors annually find good hotel accommodations and enjoy an average annual temperature of 82° F. There are good airline connections to the U.S.A., Canada and other Caribbean islands.

Dominica looks today very much as it did when Columbus first sighted this dramatically beautiful island on his second voyage in 1493. On it today still live some of the descendants of the Carib Indians who successfully discouraged settlement for a long time. It is the northernmost of the Windward Islands, and lies thirty miles south of Guadeloupe. The mountainous, green-clad country is a land of running waters. There are said to be 365 rivers, which have carved deep valleys and gullies. Dominica is twenty-nine miles long and sixteen miles wide, rugged in terrain and mostly undeveloped.

The French and English fought over Dominica, and both were attacked by the Caribs from their mountain retreats. The French burned down the capital town, Roseau, in 1805 and then withdrew, leaving Dominica to the English. The languages spoken today are English and a French patois. The grandeur of the scenery in Dominica is unforgettable, but it has poor roads, and the people

are poor. The highest peak is Morne Diablotin, which rises 4,747 feet and is covered with forests of mahogany, cedar and bamboo. For those who enjoy a feeling of isolation, and for the adventurous and hardy explorer, Dominica is perfect.

Roseau, the capital, is perched on the slopes. It is the island's principal settlement, rather than Portsmouth on the coast, which was once malarial. The malaria has been eradicated and the Dominicans hope to make the town a tourist development. The Botanical Gardens at Roseau are among the most interesting in the Caribbean. Nearby are twin waterfalls, Layou and Pagoua, romantic with their flying spray. Morne Valley is the home of Rose's Lime Juice. There are several hotels in Roseau and on a nearby silky black beach. There are also guest houses at the Archbold Plantation.

The magnificent back country of Dominica is for those energetic souls who do not mind hiking along paths through fern-filled rain forests. The

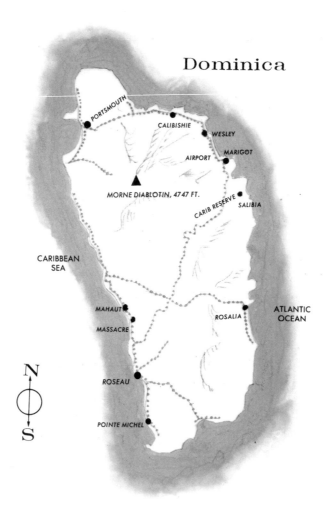

Dominica

Twentieth Century has left the people in the mountain villages almost untouched. The Trans-insular Road offers breathtaking scenery.

On the eastern coast is the Carib Reserve, where about 1,500 people of Carib blood live around a village called Salybia. Although their blood has been mixed and their language is English, they are Indian in feature. They are lively, keen-eyed and prideful. Bananas are the Caribs' principal source of income. The men build dugout canoes and the women weave baskets. There is a road to the Carib Reserve.

MARTINIQUE

An overseas department of France, this beautiful island has picturesque mountains draped with rain forests and good beaches. It covers 425 square miles, has a population of 345,000 and the language is French. Approximately 272,000 visitors, 150,000 by cruise ships, come here annually to very good hotels and resorts with superb cuisines. It is linked by air with North and South America, Europe and other Caribbean islands.

Martinique strikes the observer as having the kind of natural beauty that would inspire Gauguin. In fact, it did. Paul Gauguin painted there before he wandered on to Tahiti.

The women possess a beauty that has turned the heads of emperors. A creole lady born at Trois Îlets became the Empress of France—Josephine Bonaparte. Napoleon remarked, "I hold Martinique dear for more reasons than one." Another lady from Martinique, Francoise d'Aubigne, became Madame de Maintenon, second wife of King Louis XIV. Perhaps the most romantic bride of all was Aimée du Buc de Rivery. Born on Martinique, she attended a school in France. On the way back to her island home, the ship on which she sailed was captured by Barbary pirates. She was taken to the Grand Turk in Istanbul and made to join his harem. Soon she became Sultana, and eventually the mother of Emperor Mahmoud II.

Martinique and its people still inspire love at first sight. It is the largest and most northern of the Windward Islands, and is French in a unique way. The island contains 425 square miles of land and 345,000 people live there. The people are free and equal citizens of France. In 1946 the island became a department of France, with a prefect and all the rights and privileges of metropolitan France. The social legislation, a model for the rest of the Caribbean, provides social security, allowances to large families, and free medical care for the needy. There is little illiteracy because of the excellent primary school system throughout the island, and about ninety-five per cent of the children attend school.

Martinique is framed in magnificent blooms and tropical forests. The Carib Indians were impressed by the flowers and called the island Madinina, "Island of Flowers."

The French were the first settlers on the island in 1635, and they fought over Martinique with the British for years. The island is French today because Louis XV preferred the West Indies to Canada, and swapped the latter for the former at the Treaty of Paris in 1763.

There were two major cities on Martinique on May 7, 1902. They were St. Pierre and Fort-de-France. Then the volcano Mt. Pelée exploded the next day and destroyed St. Pierre. Thirty thousand people died in one of the worst natural disasters in history. Today the ruins of that city are the Pompeii of the Caribbean.

The capital of Martinique and the French West Indies is Fort-de-France, the quintessence of France with a Caribbean flavor. There is a fine harbor, with Fort St. Louis on one side, a green park in the center, and yellow buildings and sidewalk cafes on the other. Flowing through the town are two rivers—Rivière Madame on the north and Rivière Monsieur on the south. The balconies and the lacy iron grillwork of the city are reminiscent of old New Orleans.

Martinique

One of the largest of the Leeward Antilles, Martinique is fifty miles long and twenty-two miles wide, with a varied topography. The northern portion has rugged mountains, and here Mt. Pelée slumbers quietly. The southern half of the island is a fertile terrain with low rolling hills and green valleys. The best beaches are found along the southern shores. Ste.-Anne and Ste. Luce are magnificent long strands of coral sand backed by palms and seagrape trees. There are also good beaches near Diamant.

Martinique is primarily agricultural today. Sugar cane is the principal crop. Most people associate pineapples with Hawaii, but Columbus found this fruit on Martinique.

The heart of Fort-de-France is the Savane, the green park that runs along the waterfront. Nearby is the Caribbean Art Center, with a collection of local art and handicrafts. There are tapestries, iron sculptures, wood sculptures, tropical necklaces, creole jewelry, as well as paintings. Shops of the city, a duty-free port, offer a variety of luxuries from all over the world.

There are a number of fine hotels and good guest houses on the island, especially on the beaches near Fort-de-France. Diamond Roc, a luxurious resort just off the coast on the southern shore, has a golf course. There are also numerous family-style guest houses and attractive inns. One of the most delicious aspects of Martinique is the food, French with creole overtones.

The "joie de vivre" of the Martiniquans is marvelously evident at Carnival time. Nowhere else in the world is the spectacle more colorful, more gay. Festivals begin in mid-January, and the revelry continues until Mardi Gras. On Shrove Tuesday, floats and bands throng through the streets. Hundreds of little devils in skin-tight red costumes brandishing their pitchforks dance along behind bigger devils. The tunes tell of the devil and of Vaval's (King Bois-Bois) impending death. On Ash Wednesday Bois-Bois, king of the carnival, does die, and then the "diablesses" don costumes of black and ghostly white, with elaborate headdresses. They go about the streets mourning the death of the devil. Lilting dirges fill the air. Mardi Gras lasts twenty-four hours longer on Martinique than it does anywhere else in the world

Just south of Diamant, on the south shore of Martinique lies Rocher du Diamant (Diamond Rock), a gemlike volcano upcropping from the sea two miles from shore, rising sheer to an altitude of 573 feet.

Following orders of Sir Samuel Hood, Commodore of the Leeward Island stations, the British occupied the rock on January 7, 1804. Manned by 110 sailors and marines under Lieutenant Y.W. Maurice, the rock remained in the hands of the British for about seventeen months, falling to the French on June 29, 1805 in a highly dramatic encounter. The French were able to storm the coastline of the rock. The British retreated to the isolation of the top and staged new fortifications of the lonely rock. Soon recognizing their hopeless situation, Maurice waved the white flag of surrender. — The irony of this capitulation was that, had Maurice and his gallant band held on, they would have been relieved by Admiral Nelson, whose fleet was only hours away. But by the time Nelson's armada reached the scene, the French were on their way home with their prisoners.

ST. LUCIA

An enchanting mountainous island off the beaten track is St. Lucia, an independent state in association with Great Britain. It boasts unique scenery, safe harbors, fine beaches and excellent hotels. Through a jet airport at Vieux Fort and a smaller airport at Castries it has good airline connections to North and South America and the other islands of the West Indies. The island contains 238 square miles of land and 112,000 people who speak English and French. They host 96,000 visitors annually.

St. Lucia, for long a sleeping beauty, is now waking up and enchanting tourists. This island is endowed with great beaches and splendid mountain scenery, plus good harbors. It is 238 square miles in size. The people, who are predominantly black, speak English and French. There is an English governmental heritage and a French cultural heritage. It is an independent state in association with Great Britain.

The island was first discovered by Columbus in 1502. Caribs drove off the first Englishmen attempting settlement. The French made the first successful settlement in 1650, and thereafter St. Lucia changed hands between the British and the French fourteen times. Legacies of that fighting are forts on Morne Fortune and Vigie Hill. The island became a British colony in 1814, and is self-governing today.

St. Lucia

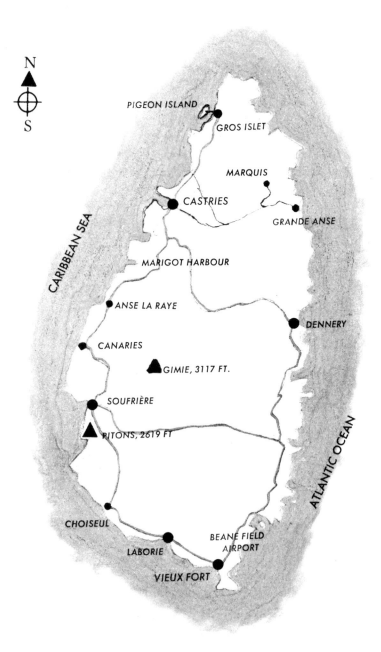

Castries, the capital and major city, has a fine deep harbor, often filled with large ships and sailing vessels. It was built after a great fire in 1948. The view from the eighteenth century Fort Charlotte is magnificent.

St. Lucia is unique in that it has a drive-in volcano, La Soufrière. It is possible to drive a car almost to the edge of the crater of this steaming, active volcano, and to walk down and watch the waters bubble and steam. Sulphur baths nearby have been used for centuries, and are famous for their curative qualities.

Two of the most outstanding landmarks of the Caribbean are St. Lucia's twin peaks, Gros Piton and Petit Piton. These spectacular spires rise straight from the sea on the leeward coast. They have been a landmark to navigators for centuries. Their steep forested sides are a challenge to experienced mountain climbers.

The Pitons are near the town of Soufrière, which is St. Lucia's second largest city, fifteen miles south of Castries on the coast. It has an attractive French colonial flavor. Diamond Baths nearby offers health baths in hot mineral springs, which are found frequently in the area.

Among the great beaches of the island is Vigie Beach, three miles of snow-white sand bathed by gin-clear water near Castries. On the northern shore is Reduit Beach, with Pigeon Island about a mile offshore connected by a causeway.

South of Castries is Marigot Bay, a fine small anchorage for yachts. The sheltered bay has a green-clad shore, clear water for snorkeling, a yacht club and hotel. Beyond the town of Vieux Fort on the southern end of the land is Anse de Sables, one of the finest beaches on the island. It is sheltered from the Atlantic surf by offshore coral reefs.

The road around St. Lucia follows the coast on the leeward side from Gros Inlet on the north to Vieux Fort at the southern end, sometimes going up in the foothills, sometimes dipping down to the sea. It swings north again along the Atlantic side and continues up the coast to Dennery. There the road goes inland and crosses the mountains to reach Castries again. The drive is one of the most delightful in the West Indies.

Today St. Lucia is alive with plans to attract tourists. For some years it has been a favorite port-of-call for cruising yachtsmen, but an increasing number of visitors are coming, and more and more accommodations are being built for them. There is good airline service. The pleasant atmosphere, with its French flavor, the magnificent scenery and the fine beaches are the endowments that assure St. Lucia a rising tide of guests.

BARBADOS

A sovereign state and member of the British Commonwealth, this hilly island has large sugar cane plantations, elegant resorts and hotels, beautiful beaches. The size is 166 square miles, the population, 260,000, and the capital, Bridgetown, with a deepwater harbor. Recreational facilities include a race track, golf courses, yacht clubs, tennis courts, cricket fields and fishing for wahoo, tarpon, tuna, dolphin and bonito. Barbados is famous for flying fish. There are direct airline connections with North and South America, Europe and other Caribbean islands. Visitors number 342,000 annually, with 100,000 arriving by cruise ships. The language is English.

Barbados has been beloved by sun-seekers for several centuries. Indeed, George Washington slept here, when he brought his brother, Lawrence, to the island to recuperate from tuberculosis. Barbados is the only land outside North America on which Washington ever set foot. One of the island's charming hotels dates back to 1878, and is still in operation. Many elegant resorts and tourist accommodations have been added since then.

This small island has a quiet, cultivated countryside that suggests southern England transplanted to the tropics. It has always been British, and its Old World charm is British to the core. Combine an eighteenth century atmosphere with a benign climate, many miles of white sand beaches, interesting villages in rolling hills and you have the secret of Barbados.

Bridgetown is the capital, and it has a fine deep water harbor. Here there is a Trafalgar Square with a statue of Lord Nelson that is twenty-seven years older than London's statue of that hero of Trafalgar Bay. Harbor policemen are dressed as Nelson's sailors were in bell-bottom trousers, white pullover shirts and flat straw boaters. This is a lively town, and on the streets handsome black politicians, Portuguese merchants, turbaned Hindus, Venezuelan oil men and prosperous planters rub elbows. Moving about among the men on the careenage docks are the Mauby women, who pass about selling mauby-bark beer.

Things to see in Bridgetown include the George Washington House, where he stayed when he visited in 1751, and the seventeenth century St.

Barbados

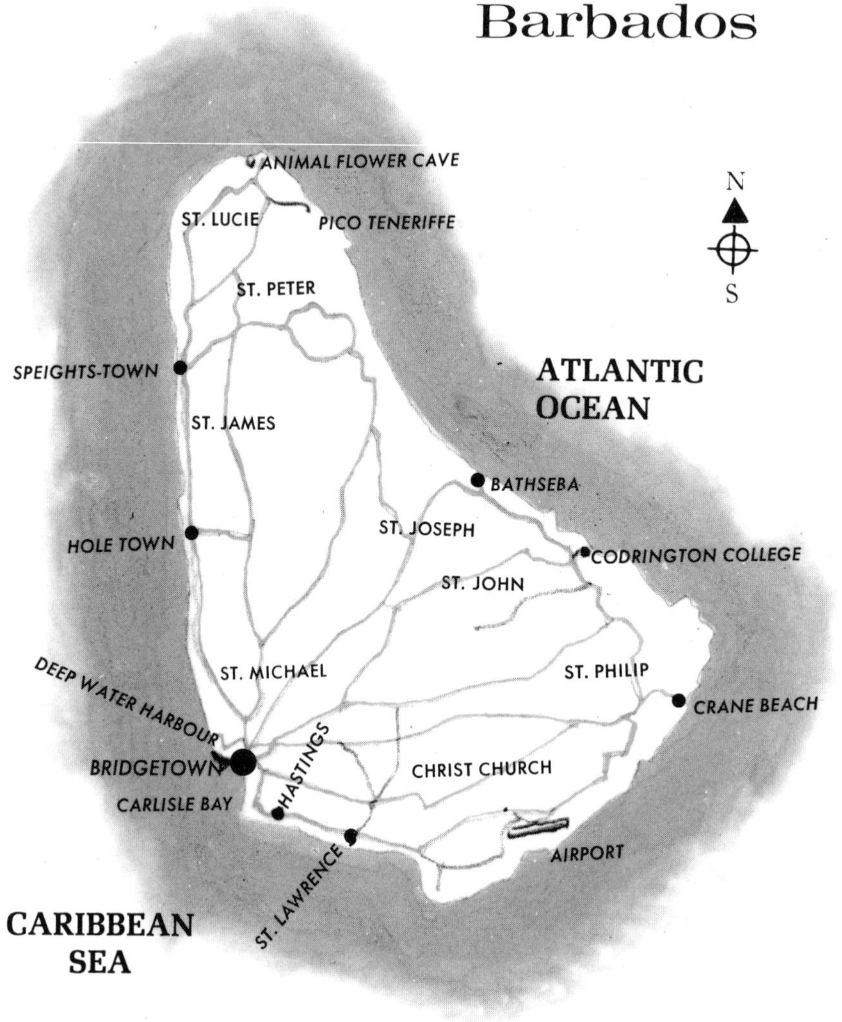

ANIMAL FLOWER CAVE

ST. LUCIE   PICO TENERIFFE

ST. PETER

SPEIGHTS-TOWN

ST. JAMES

HOLE TOWN

ST. JOSEPH

BATHSEBA

CODRINGTON COLLEGE

ST. JOHN

ATLANTIC OCEAN

DEEP WATER HARBOUR

ST. MICHAEL

ST. PHILIP

CRANE BEACH

BRIDGETOWN

HASTINGS

CHRIST CHURCH

CARLISLE BAY

ST. LAWRENCE

AIRPORT

CARIBBEAN SEA

Michael's Cathedral. In nearby Garrison is the Barbados Museum, with historical material of the island.

Good, though narrow, roads encircle the island and crisscross through the hills. The east coast on the Atlantic, and the west coast on the Caribbean are equally attractive, but quite different. On the Atlantic coast is Sam Lord's Castle, a splendid plantation house built in 1830. Today it is an elegant resort with a beautiful beach.

The shores become steeper to the north and here the Atlantic pounds the rocks with huge breakers. Bathsheba is the home of the Flying Fish Fleet, and it is also an attractive windward resort. From the village of Tent Bay nearby the brightly painted fleet sets out almost every day to net flying fish, which are considered the tastiest treat Barbados has to offer. They are practically the emblem of the island.

The western, leeward coast of Barbados is

sheltered from the pounding surf. It is known as the "platinum coast," the Riviera of Barbados. Both shores have magnificent, soft, white sand beaches, but the clear Caribbean is far gentler than the Atlantic. On this side of the island is Speightstown, the second largest city on Barbados. The center of the elegant and exclusive resort area is St. James. The western shore contains a variety of accommodations, ranging from modest to luxurious resorts. North of Bridgetown on the western shore there are more than a dozen superb resorts, and there are equally as many to the south of the capital. There is a social cachet to wintering in Barbados that keeps these resorts nicely filled.

Among the interesting sights along the western shore is one of the oldest churches in the New World, built in 1684 at St. James. Freshwater Bay, in the Parish of St. Michael, has freshwater springs appearing in the sand of Paradise Beach, which curves round the bay. At the end of this beach is the ruin of an old fort. A new resort hotel has been built overlooking Carlisle Bay on Needham's Point.

Barbados has the distinction of being the only island in the West Indies that was colonized by the English that did not change hands. The first British settlers were gentlemen farmers who, with their slaves, landed in 1625, and no other nation has ever seized control. From early years till now sugar cane has been the principal crop.

One of the curious stories of Barbados is the tale of the "Redlegs." These were white indentured servants from Scotland who were sold into what was, in effect, slavery in the West Indies after they rebelled unsuccessfully against James II of England. Blond, blue-eyed "Redlegs," so-called from the knees their ancestors displayed in Scottish kilts, today live inland from Bathsheba in the beautiful "Scottish Highlands" of Barbados.

Sports are dear to Barbadians. Cricket is their favorite game, and some native players enjoy fame throughout the cricket-playing world. From July through December is the season for polo-playing. The horse-loving British have also seen to it that there is first-rate horse racing at Garrison Savannah. Islanders and visitors find that the rolling country with its beautiful views of the sea is perfect for exploration on horseback. There are two golf courses on the island and numerous tennis courts. Football, basketball and netball are also popular. Every kind of water sport can be enjoyed. The clear, quiet waters of the west and southern coast are sheltered by coral reefs, and offer fine underwater sight-seeing. Fishing is good, especially from February to May when the migrating schools pass by. Small boats can be rented; yachts chartered.

Barbados, with the patina it has acquired as a retreat of the wealthy and famous, has an Edwardian flavor. This is attractive also to those who are not wealthy or famous. The combination of these visitors, plus the important agricultural production, makes this one of the more prosperous islands in the Caribbean.

ST. VINCENT

An independent state with full internal self government, associated with the United Kingdom, this beautiful volcanic island is eighteen miles long, eleven miles wide. It has palm-lined beaches, good roads, and a population of 94,000, including a Carib Indian settlement. The average temperature is about 83° F. annually, the average rainfall about ninety inches. The main income of the island is from agricultural products: arrowroot, bananas, cassava and sea island cotton. There are a few good hotels with golf, tennis and croquet. The capital is Kingstown, which has a deepwater harbor. The language is English. Tourism draws 40,000 visitors annually, 22,000 of them on cruise ships.

St.Vincent

St. Vincent has the reputation of being the most cheerful and festive of the Windward Islands. Among its other distinctions is that it exports millions of tons of arrowroot starch each year to the United States, and it has a breadfruit tree growing in Kingstown's Botanical Gardens from a seed brought back by Captain Bligh from Tahiti. St. Vincent is said to resemble Tahiti. It is a beautiful island eighteen miles long and eleven miles wide, with palm-lined beaches and good roads. Rivers, streams and waterfalls lace the forested mountain slopes. The volcano, Soufrière, 4,000 feet high, is the highest peak and a blue lake is cupped in its cloud-shrouded crater.

The Caribs called this island Haroun, "Land of the Blessed." St. Vincent and Dominica are the only two islands in the West Indies where one can meet Caribs today. This is indeed a melting pot. The English, the French, and the Caribs alternated in fighting one another. The English finally won. The language is English, but many of the people are of French descent. In addition there are Black Caribs, Africans, Portuguese and East Indians.

Green hills rise behind the red roofs of Kingstown, the principal city. St. Vincent's Botanical

Gardens are the oldest in the Caribbean. It was the poverty of St. Vincent that caused the British Crown to send Captain Bligh on the Bounty to bring back breadfruit, which is a staple food. From Kingstown there is a road that winds eight hundred feet up to the ruins of Fort Charlotte. This was built by the British in the early years of the nineteenth century, and offers a fine view over the city to the sea.

South of Kingstown is Caliaqua, an attractive area with nice beaches. Just offshore is tiny Young Island, with fine beaches beneath rocky cliffs. Here is an elegant resort hidden away in the tropical vegetation. The neat grounds are pastoral, and there is a delightful pool overhung with flowers and ferns.

Snorkeling, skin-diving, fishing and mountain-climbing are among the daytime activities of the visitors who have been lucky enough to discover St. Vincent. At night there is dancing and music, from time to time with combos from Trinidad. The hotels are restful and attractive. This beautiful little island, fragrant with flowers, is a place for restoring the soul with simple pleasures.

THE GRENADINES

This beautiful group of over 100 little islands lies between St. Vincent and Grenada. The largest of the islands are Bequia and Carriacou. Several islands have air strips and there are good small hotels and cottage colonies. The Grenadines are a paradise for sailing, fishing and diving. The language is English.

There are hundreds of Grenadines, if rocks and reefs are included. However, there are only about 125 islands strung out along this chain throughout seventy miles of the Caribbean between St. Vincent and Grenada that are large enough to deserve the name. On these dots of land, the peaks of volcanic mountains emerging from the sea, live some fourteen thousand people, and most make their living from the sea. Only ten of the islands have a permanent population. They are truly outposts of civilization. All are English in government. Most of them are associated with St. Vincent. Grenada administers a few of the islets and Carriacou at the southern end of the string. The inhabitants speak English.

Bequia, northernmost of the group, is nine miles south of St. Vincent. On this island Admiralty Harbor is a safe, sheltered anchorage, and the village facing the harbor, Port Elizabeth, is delightful. Soft white beaches stretch away on all sides, and Princess Margaret Beach is one of the prettiest in the Caribbean. The village consists of a few small inns, a few small stores, a few churches, and a small hospital. The atmosphere is idyllic.

The people who live on these islands are great boat-builders, and native sails ply the waters in inter-island trade. On a number of the Grenadines the French, the first settlers, set their stamp. The local patois has a French flavor, and there are

The Grenadines

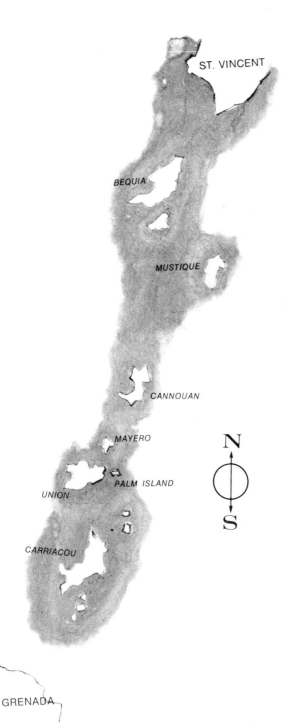

remains of some great plantation houses, forts and old stone structures.

South of Bequia are little unoccupied islets—Battowia, Petit Nevis, Baleceaux, Quartre. Next comes Mustique, which is being developed as a private and exclusive resort. The next large island is Cannouan, which has good harbors at Grand Bay and Charles Bay. Then come the Tiny Tobago Cays, and Mayreau, a larger island with high hills and a few hundred inhabitants.

Union Island's thousand foot mountain is a landmark. There is a road here that climbs to an old French fort, good anchorages, and inns in the village of Clifton. Palm Island, once Prune Island, is being developed by an American as an attractive cottage-resort. It has an airstrip with frequent scheduled flights. Petit St. Vincent is a small, civilized island with a handsome inn, guest cottages and boats for sailing and fishing. The largest island in the Grenadines is Carriacou, which has miles of good roads, an airfield and an attractive inn.

Grenada

GRENADA

An independent state associated with the United Kingdom, this is "The Spice Island of the West", and spices are the main industry. Grenada offers beautiful mountain scenery, good beaches, excellent hotel accommodations. In size it is 120 square miles. The population numbers 110,000, and the capital, St. Georges, has 10,000 inhabitants. There are good airline connections to North and South America and to other Caribbean islands. Vacationers enjoy golf, tennis, fishing, yacht club facilities. English is the language. Approximately 110,000 visitors arrive annually, and of these 86,000 come on cruise ships.

Grenada has mountains mantled in green, lush tropical valleys, magnificent beaches, and a leisurely, sweet atmosphere. It also has a race track, good roads, excellent resort accommodations, art galleries, golf courses, tennis courts and movies. The island has absorbed these elements of civilization in a delightful fashion.

Grenada is known as the "Spice Island of the West," and the air is fragrant with the smell of cinnamon, vanilla, ginger, mayberry and nutmeg. Almost a third of the world's spices are grown here. St. George, the port and chief city, is one of the most delightful little towns in the Caribbean. This toylike town sits on a hill beside the excellent harbor. Pastel-painted, red-roofed houses have outer staircases, fan-shaped windows and wrought-iron balconies. Though Grenada is one of the British Windward Islands, it has a French flavor.

Grand Anse Beach, one of the finest in the Caribbean, is about a mile from St. George. Excellent hotels rise beside the shining sand along this two-mile beach. Among the other pleasant places to visit are the colorful markettowns of Grenville and Goyave, the beaches at Pointe Saline, Levera Beach, and the pretty homes at Westerhall Point, a narrow peninsular where eight hundred poinciana trees have been planted. Halifax Harbour is a snug inlet that offers shelter to boatmen in storms, and has a nice beach inn.

The Dougaldston Estate near Charlotte Town is fascinating. Charlotte Town is a shipping center for spices, stored in ancient stone buildings. At the Dougaldston Estate the visitor can see nutmegs, allspice, cloves, black pepper, cinnamon, touca beans, bay leaves, vanilla and cocoa beans growing and being processed.

The mountainous interior of the island is as delightful as the shore line. Roads and paths lead into a dramatic landscape, complete with waterfalls, orchids, and an occasional funny little monkey. A road leads to the top of Grand Etang, a volcanic crater with a lake in the crater. Paths through lovely woodlands filled with flowers wind round to Annandale Falls.

For more ambitious mountain climbers there is Mount St. Catherine, the highest peak on the island, and Mt. Qua Qua. Julien Fedón, a mulatto planter who led a bloody rebellion against the English, made his headquarters on Mt. Qua Qua. It was also here he finally surrendered. Near the town of Sauteurs the Indians who first lived on Grenada threw themselves into the sea when threatened with capture by the French.

TRINIDAD

United with Tobago, Trinidad is an independent state within the British Commonwealth, a member of the United Nations, of the Organization of American States, and of the Caribbean Free Trade Association. It is 1,864 square miles in size and has beautiful mountain scenery and some good beaches. Trinidad is famous as the home of the steel band, and for a festive carnival. The capital, Port-of-Spain, has 95,000 inhabitants. The chief industries are the production of asphalt, rum, margarine, soap, sugar, coffee, cocoa and coconuts. There are several good hotels, most of them in Port-of-Spain. The population of 1,080,000 includes many different races—East Indians, Chinese, Africans, English, French and Spanish. Sports include golf, sailing, tennis, fishing for red snapper, mackerel and tarpon, horse racing, cricket and hockey. There are numerous good nightclubs. The languages are English and Spanish. There are good airline connections to North America, South America, Europe and other Caribbean islands.

Southernmost of the Caribbean islands, Trinidad is only sixteen miles off the coast of Venezuela. The mountainous island has peaks more than 3,000 feet above sea level, and seven lovely rivers that keep the fertile land green with forests and farms. Pitch Lake, one of the largest asphalt lakes in the world, is a peerless phenomenon that covers one hundred acres and is nearly three hundred feet deep. Asphalt from this lake covers the highways of the world.

When Columbus discovered Trinidad on his third voyage he found Arawaks living here in settled villages, making music with drums and conch shell horns. In 1592 the first permanent settlement was established by Spaniards in the town of St. Joseph on the Caroni River. It was later sacked by Sir Walter Raleigh. The French from Haiti and other French islands moved in by the thousands in 1780, the year of the slaves' revolution in Haiti, at the invitation of Spain's King Charles III. The British captured the island in 1797, and British it remained thereafter. In 1962 it became an independent nation within the British Commonwealth.

Trinidad

Map of Trinidad showing VENEZUELA, Maracas Bay, BLANCHISSEUSE, TOCO, Galera Point, Northern Range, ST. JOSEPH, ARIMA, VALENCIA, Matura Bay, PORT OF SPAIN, PIARCO Airport, CHAGUANAS, COUVA, Central Range, Cocos Bay, GULF OF PARIA, SAN FERNANDO, RIO CLARO, LA BREA, PITCH LAKE, PRINCES TOWN, Mayaro Bay, FYZABAD Oil Wells, ATLANTIC OCEAN

With the abolition of slavery in 1838, many thousands of East Indians were brought in to work the fields, and additional thousands of laborers came from China, Portugal and other West Indian islands. The mixture of people on the island is remarkable, and it has been claimed that all the na-3tions of the world are represented here. In this fascinating collection of mixed races English is the language of most of the people. But in the mountainous northern portion Spanish, a Spanish patois, French, and a French patois are also spoken.

Trinidad gave the world the steel band. They are direct descendants of the voodoo drums of Africa. These unique bands evolved from the "Tamboo-Bamboo" Carnivals, which for years fostered the native musical skill of the African islanders. Musicians beat rhythms by knocking together pieces of bamboo, while merrymakers chanted tunes. Today the steel drums have been fairly well standardized. They range from full-sized forty-four gallon oil drums to the Ping Pong, a drum cut to about six inches from the top.

The island is also recognized as the home of calypso, the folk songs of Afro-West Indian. Calypso is poetry and song, witty and satirical. It serves as town crier and village gossip as well as rich entertainment.

Today Trinidad is the most industrialized and wealthiest island in the Caribbean. Sugar cane, cocoa, rice, bananas, citrus fruits, copra and many forest products are exported. Asphalt is a major export, and the island is today the second largest source of oil in the British Commonwealth, with a large Texaco refinery near San Fernando. Trinidad also has a good supply of natural gas. Chemical industries, a modern soap factory and a paint plant are among the many industries that have in recent years located in Trinidad. They have been lured there both by the availability of industrial fuel and by special tax concessions designed to encourage local and foreign investment. In the last decade large sums have been spent to improve harbors, roads, bridges, water supply, land drainage and reclamation, electricity production and housing.

The island is mountainous in its northern range, which extends from east to west. In the center are the Montserrat Hills and in the south the Trinity Hills. The rest of the country is fertile flat land.

There are excellent hotels and resort accommodations in Port-of-Spain, the capital, and nearby Maraval and on some of the island's superb beaches. Almost all of the beaches are accessible by good roads. Port-of-Spain is a fascinating city to explore, and is especially exciting at carnival time. Here there are mosques, Victorian mansions, and other architectural structures and styles in the private homes on the Savannah, which is the two hundred acre Central Park of the city. The Savannah is the setting for the festive carnivals.

Cricket, a favorite sport in Trinidad, is played in Queen's Park Oval, which can hold thirty thousand spectators. St. Andrews Golf Course, founded in 1890, is world famous. It is at Maraval and has two eighteen-hole courses. There is a nine-hole course at La Brea. There are three horse-racing tracks—at Port-of-Spain, San Fernando and Arima. Small game is hunted on the island, which is well stocked with deer, wild hog, alligators, mongooses, and certain game birds.

The favorite beaches are at Maracas Bay and Las Cuevas Bay—fine for swimming, surfboarding and water-skiing. These beaches are on the northern coast, and are reached by the Skyline Highway, a scenic drive with grand views. The Saddle Drive curves through graceful bamboos, citrus groves, cocoa and coffee plantations, and overlooks the capital from the heights. In the Blue Basin, a two-and-a-half hour round trip from Port-of-Spain, is a beautiful pond fed by a very high waterfall. On the east coast are miles of beaches, coves and lush tropical vegetation.

Bird lovers will enjoy a trip to the Caroni Swamp, where the rare scarlet ibis may be seen. Visitors are only allowed in this bird sanctuary between July and September. Among the other places of interest on the island are Mount St. Benedict, a hilltop monastery; the Shrine of the Black Virgin at the Church of La Divina Pastora at Siparia, and the Shrine of Our Lady of Laventille in the hills northeast of Port-of-Spain.

Tobago

Map labels: CHARLOTTE VILLE, LITTLE TOBAGO, CASTARA, SPEYSIDE, MORIAH, PLYMOUTH, MASON HALL, KING'S BAY, PIGEON POINT, SCARBOROUGH, MILFORD, CROWN POINT AIRPORT, COLUMBUS PT, N, S

TOBAGO

Tobago and Trinidad form one independent state within the British Commonwealth. This romantic, mountainous island covers 117 square miles, has good roads, fine hotels, beautiful beaches, interesting bird life and splendid submarine scenes. The population is 37,000, the language English. There are good airline links with North America and other Caribbean islands.

Tobago is a simple island, with natural beauty and an unsophisticated charm. This mountainous island has good beaches, beautiful views, doll-like villages and the golden-feathered Greater Bird of Paradise. This is the last stand of that rare and magnificent bird. Tobago is also said to be the legendary home of Robinson Crusoe and his man Friday, and Crusoe's cave is said to be located on a most beautiful and desolate beach.

Tobago was not always as peaceful as it is today. It changed hands thirty-one times. The Spaniards who settled nearby Trinidad ignored it. The Dutch, the French, the English, natives of the Duchy of Courland (now Latvia), and pirates fought over it. At one time in the eighteenth century it was agreed that Tobago would remain a no-man's land, and pirates moved in for a while. The English first settled on Tobago in 1763 and planted sugar cane. It became an English possession in 1803. Tobago was a ward of Trinidad until, along with Trinidad, it became in 1962 an independent member of the British Commonwealth.

Scarborough, the capital, is on the southeastern shore facing the Atlantic, and most of the hotels are on that side of the island. The quaint town fronts on Rockly Bay and is backed by hills. North of Scarborough on the windward coast are pleasant little fishing villages—Mount St. George, Pembroke, Roxborough, Delaford and Speyside. Two small islands lie offshore from Speyside, and the bigger is called Little Tobago or Bird of Paradise Island. It was to this island that Sir William Ingram in 1912 brought the Birds of Paradise that were originally native to the Aru Islands of New Guinea, where they were threatened with extinction by plume hunters. He gave Little Tobago to the Government as a permanent sanctuary.

The road curves across the hills in the northern part of the island to Charlottesville, which has a good beach, and then follows the coast south to Plymouth and Crown Point. There are fine beaches on the Caribbean side at Store Bay, Great Courland Bay and Buccoo.

Tobago's Buccoo Reef off the southwest coast is one of the most beautiful coral reefs in the Caribbean. There are fish-filled coral canyons exotic in design, in warm, crystal-clear water that tempt the snorkeler to hang above them for hours. There are also evidences of old ship-wrecks, which conjure up the possibilities of pirate treasures under the sands.

The island's airport is on the southern end near Crown Point, which has a splendid beach, two tennis courts, and a good hotel. There is also another hotel at Arnos Vale Beach on a cove beside the Caribbean.

At one period in the last century the island was a booming sugar producer, but when the market for that crop failed the planters sold their land to their former slaves and the great plantation houses fell to ruins. Today Tobago's main crops are cocoa and coconuts. Tropical fruits, vegetables, coffee, bananas, sweet potatoes, some sugar, breadfruit trees and cashew nuts are also raised.

At Little Courland there is an elegant residential community, Mount Irvine. It has an eighteen-hole golf course, a hotel, swimming pool, and a beach on the Caribbean.

MARGARITA

MARGARITA

This most interesting and beautiful island, with its old towns and churches, quiet coves and beautiful beaches, belongs to Venezuela. It is noted for pearl diving in surrounding waters, and great carnival and folklore festivals. The language is Spanish.

For those who have dreamed of pearl-diving in pellucid waters, Margarita is the island. A fortune has been brought up in pearl oysters from the sea around Margarita. This is a Spanish island, in language and culture, linked to Venezuela by ferry and by an aqueduct that brings water from Cumana on the mainland. It is also linked by government.

It is as much fun to explore the land of Margarita as it is the water around it. Small colonial Spanish villages, fertile valleys, flocks of scarlet ibis along the waterways, ancient churches, beautiful beaches tempt the adventurer to wander about.

The principal town is Porlamar, near the airport. This is a vivid, colorful town, especially at carnival time in February, and from May through September, when there are music and folklore festivals, yacht regattas, and fiestas. Christmas here is celebrated with traditional and wonderful bird and fish dances.

The roads round the island are good, passing beside a peaceful beach at El Morro, through a fishing village, Bella Vista, and Pampatar, with its colonial church. The capital town is La Asunción, on the coast north of Porlamar. Founded in 1562, it is an attractive Spanish colonial city with a great Cathedral, a museum, the Government palace, ruins of ancient buildings and a palm-lined square.

Several dozen pleasant hotels are scattered about Margarita. The beaches and the skin diving could not be better. Cockfighting is a favorite local sport. The food is wonderful, the fishing fine. Margarita is distinctive and delightful.

BONAIRE

Second largest of the Dutch A B C islands, Bonaire covers 112 square miles and has a population of 8,500. Though it is near Curacao, it lies off the beaten path. Among the interesting bird life is a big flamingo colony. The clear water around the island has splendid coral and other marine life. There are good accommodations in the capital, Kralendijk. Airline connections are available via Curaçao. The languages are Dutch, English and Papiamento. Of the 14,000 visitors annually, 4,500 come on cruise ships.

Amerigo Matteo Vespucci, who gave his name to America, was the navigator of the Spanish ship that first landed on Bonaire. There the Spaniards found an abundance of dye-wood and turtles. Bonaire is derived from the name that the Indian inhabitants gave the island, and means "the low country." This low island fifty miles off the coast of Venezuela is one of the four autonomous island territories of the Netherlands Antilles, the others being Aruba, Curaçao and the Windward Islands. Curaçao, twenty miles to the west, is Bonaire's nearest neighbor.

Bonaire is enormously appealing, especially to skin-divers and bird-lovers. Here thousands of flamingos mate and nest annually. They feed in shallow lagoons at both ends of the island, especially at Great Salt Lake on the southern side. The road to the lake passes old slave huts and salt pans where slaves once harvested salt. In addition to the dramatically beautiful flamingos there are thousands of green parrots, parakeets, warbirds, herons, terns, pelicans and other tropical species.

The waters round Bonaire are just as rewarding to skin-divers and spearfishermen. International spearfishing tournaments have been held here. There is a big land-locked bay, called the Lac, that is ideal for spearfishing. The island has

Continued on page 124

Description of the following pictures

page 105
GRENADA: THE HARBOR OF ST. GEORGE'S
Grenada is one of the most beautiful scenic islands of the West Indies. Its capital, St. George's, is situated on a craggy peninsula spectacularly colorful, with red-and-white houses, green hills and the azure waters of the harbor. Its streets are almost medievally narrow and twisting. Government offices now occupy Fort George, which was built in 1705 by the French. Just south of the city is Grand Anse, Grenada's famous beach.

page 106
CURAÇAO: NATIVE SINGERS AND MUSICIANS
The people of Curaçao cultivate the traditions of their island, wearing old custumes, and preserving traditional music and dances. The couple on the left is a member of a folklore group of singers and dancers who perform from time to time in the city. The musicians to the right use some of the old traditional instruments of the island.

CURAÇAO: BREEDESTRAAT, BUSINESS STREET IN WILLEMSTAD
Breedestraat is the elegant shopping street in Willemstad, capital of the island. The building to the left, with the bells, is the home of Spritzer & Fuhrmann, famous jeweller of Curaçao. Many fine stores are on this street: Penha, Wooden Shoe, Kan Jewelers, Van Dorp, Casa Amarilla, El Globo, New Amsterdam Store, Salas and others. The street has a colorful line of old Dutch houses interspersed with modern structures which harmonize with the old ones.

page 107
WILLEMSTAD: CAPITAL OF CURAÇAO
Uniquely Dutch and definitely European is the city of Willemstad. The picture shows some of the ancient fortifications with the waterfront to the right. This fortress has been converted into a modern hotel of imposing dimensions. The city faces the Caribbean Sea. To the left is St. Anna Bay, with the Queen Emma Pontoon Bridge leading to the city section of Punda, visible in the picture, from Otrobanda on the other side of the bay.

QUEEN JULIANA BRIDGE, CURAÇAO
Like a tremendous arch the new Queen Juliana Bridge overlooks the capital city, leading over St. Anna Bay and connecting Otrobanda with Punda. In front of the photograph is Punda with Fort Amsterdam, now modernized to Government offices, behind St. Anna Bay and in the background Otrobanda. Just under the bridge a big tanker passes through St. Anna Bay.

page 108
ARUBA: THE HARBOR OF ORANJESTAD (PAARDEN BAY)
Oranjestad is the capital and largest town on the island. It is situated on the leeward coast and has a fine natural deep-water harbor. The port of Oranjestad is the commercial harbor of Aruba, well-protected by a coral reef and open day and night. The picture shows the town of Oranjestad in the background.

ARUBA: COUNTRYSIDE AND THE OLDE MOLEN (OLD WINDMILL)
An authentic Dutch windmill, originally built in Holland in 1815, was brought to Aruba and rebuilt to be used as an attractive restaurant. The picture also shows a typical view of Aruba's cunucu (countryside) scenery, with numerous cacti, opuntias and cerei, and a few palms in the background.

ARUBA: THE FAMOUS BEACH
On the sheltered western coast of Aruba, where there are luxurious resort hotels; the island is fringed by what seems to be an unending beach of snow-white sand. One beach follows the other, on and on. Among the most beautiful is Palm Beach, where this picture was taken.

Continued on page 121

THE HARBOR OF ST. GEORGE'S, GRENADA

NATIVE SINGERS AND MUSICIANS

CURAÇAO

BREEDESTRAAT, BUSINESS STREET IN WILLEMSTAD

WILLEMSTAD,
CAPITAL OF CURAÇAO

CURAÇAO

QUEEN JULIANA BRIDGE
OVER ST. ANNA BAY

HARBOR OF ORANJESTAD
(PAARDEN BAY)

COUNTRYSIDE AND
THE OLDE MOLEN (WINDMILL)

ARUBA

For detailed description see page 104

THE FAMOUS BEACH

PALM BEACH WITH
ARUBA CARIBBEAN HOTEL

NATURAL BRIDGE
BIGGEST IN CARIBBEAN

ARUBA

ANCIENT INDIAN POTTERY

FLAMINGO COLONY:
PARENTS, CHILDREN, EGGS

For detailed description see page 121

BONAIRE

GOTO MEER WITH
BRANDARIS HILL

SECLUDED BEACH

110

PORT ANTONIO

*RAFTING ON
RIO GRANDE*

JAMAICA.

For detailed description see page 121

111

CALYPSO
GROUP

DRAMATIC ART

JAMAICAN
FOLKLORE

For detailed description see page 121

LIMBO DANCERS

DUNN'S
RIVER
FALLS

OCHO
RIOS
JAMAICA

GEORGETOWN, CAPITAL OF CAYMAN ISLANDS

GRAND CAYMAN ISLAND

WRECKS AT THE REEF OF GRAND CAYMAN

For detailed description see page 122

THE SEVEN MILE BEACH

THE CAPITOL IN HAVANA

CUBA

ROMAN CATHOLIC CATHEDRAL HAVANA

IN THE SUGAR CANE FIELDS, LAS VILLAS

RUINS OF SANS SOUCI
PALACE AT MILOT

HAÏTI

For detailed description see page 122

HAITI'S FAMOUS PRIMITIVE ARTISTS

INTERIOR, ALCAZAR DE COLÓN (1510)
SANTO DOMINGO

→

TOMB OF CHRISTOPHER COLUMBUS
IN SANTO DOMINGO

DOMINICAN REPUBLIC

NATIVE ART EXPOSITION

CARIBBEAN MOON NIGHT

Description of the foregoing pictures continued from page 104

page 109

PALM BEACH WITH CARIBBEAN HOTEL

In front of the photograph is Aruba's famous Palm Beach, with the Aruba Caribbean Hotel and part of the beach (right) of the Aruba Sheraton. Behind is the cunucu, a desert-like countryside with cacti, aloes, divi-divi trees and several small villages. This countryside has known gold-mining, and gold can still be found on the surface in gullies and valleys of the island.

NATURAL BRIDGE, ARUBA

Aruba's Natural Bridge is the biggest and highest in the Caribbean. The reddish rock of the bridge contrasts dramatically with the blue-black cliffs in the foreground. It is located near Andicouri on the north coast of the island. The erosion of the rocks by the wind-driven rushing waters that carved the bridge still continues. It is one of the great sights of Aruba.

ANCIENT INDIAN POTTERY AND FIRESTONES, ARUBA

Before the arrival of the white man, Aruba was populated by friendly Indians, who left many relics of their primitive culture, such as the stone axes and pottery pictured here. The Indians were not exterminated on this island, as they were throughout the rest of the Caribbean. On the contrary, the island was considered somewhat as an Indian reservation. This policy resulted in amicable race relations, and Arubans today are a mixture of Indian with Spanish and Dutch blood of the early colonists.

page 110

FLAMINGO COLONY: PARENTS, CHILDREN AND EGGS, BONAIRE

Bonaire is not only residence but also breeding place of a large colony of several thousand flamingos. The photograph gives an impressive view of such a breeding place with nests and eggs in the foreground, young (gray) birds in the middle-ground and brilliant pink parents flying over them.

BONAIRE: GOTO MEER WITH BRANDARIS HILL

Going inland the most scenic part of Bonaire is in the north around Goto Meer, a large lake surrounded by hills. In the background of the picture the highest point of the island, Brandaris Hill, 784 ft. high, is visible.

SECLUDED BEACH, BONAIRE

Bonaire is an island with only a few hotels but many beautiful beaches. This picture was taken on the west shore not far north of Kralendijk.

page 111

JAMAICA: PORT ANTONIO

This is Jamaica—high mountains, lush green vegetation, good harbors, palm-framed beaches, friendly villages, and, all around, the clear, blue waters of the Caribbean Sea. The photograph depicts one of the loveliest areas of Jamaica, a section of the northeast coast. Here, nature has been at her most lavish and beautiful vistas abound. The view shows the twin harbors of Port Antonio, with the town on the peninsula separating the two bays.

JAMAICA: RAFTING ON RIO GRANDE

A unique sport on Jamaica is river-rafting. This is done on the Rio Grande near Port Antonio and is enjoyed by many visitors. The trip is made downstream on rafts that are completely safe, with only mild thrills when the rafts "shot the rapids." Swimming and fishing are also part of the adventure.

page 112

JAMAICAN FOLKLORE

Jamaica developed its own forms of Caribbean music and dances, especially calypso and limbo. This individual flavor is also expressed in the different costumes shown in the pictures. The folksongs give a vivid Africanized version of English ballads, rich in humor, imagery, wit and satire. A dramatic art developed especially well in Jamaica is pantomime. Scenes like the one pictured in the photograph are performed with native music by local groups in hotels. The Little Theatre Movement has spearheaded the establishment of a Jamaican Theater.

Continued from page 103

great white sand beaches, and beachcombers can enjoy collecting conchs. Spiny lobster are found in the shallow waters along the coast, and a fine variety of game fish may be caught or speared offshore.

The capital is Kralendijk, Dutch for "Coral Dike." It is a quaint little spic-and-span Dutch town in the Caribbean style. Sailing vessels come into the small harbor for the fish market on the docks, and this is a pleasant place to stroll and inspect their catches. Kralendijk is on the western coast of the island. Opposite the town is Little Bonaire, a small uninhabited islet that is a pleasant picnic spot for sailing parties.

This tranquil island has good roads from end to end, an airport, and excellent hotel accommodations. It also has a gambling casino, part of recent government efforts to lure tourists. The hotels are on wide, white beaches and have water sports facilities.

Rincon, in the center of the island, is the only village on Bonaire. At Rincon the villagers attend Birds' Mass or "Misa de Para." This is the Mass that is read, when the maize is on the stalk, early in the morning so that the people can be in the field at sunrise to shoo away the birds that come to eat the crop.

After Vespucci's visit to Bonaire only a few Spaniards settled on the island, mostly exiles from Venezuela. The Dutch came in 1636, cut some of the abundant dye-wood and brought in slaves to harvest salt and raise herds of cattle and horses. England ruled the island briefly in the early years of the nineteenth century, and leased the whole island to a New Yorker. Fortunately he did not cut

all the trees on the island, though timber was an export. Bonaire was returned to Holland after a few years.

The official language of Bonaire is Dutch. The popular language is Papiamento, which is also spoken on Aruba and Curaçao. It is a language that originated with Portuguese slave traders, and contains Spanish, Dutch, African and English elements. Though all the natives speak Papiamento, nobody agrees on the spelling of the words.

CURAÇAO

Largest of the islands of the Netherlands Antilles, Curaçao contains 179 square miles and has a population of 145,000. Willemstad, the capital, is famous as a freeport and as one of the busiest ports of the world. Hotel accommodations are excellent. The climate is dry, with an average temperature of 81° F. There are good beaches, golf, fishing, sailing and excellent airline connections to North and South America, Europe and other Caribbean islands. The languages are Dutch, English, Spanish and Papiamento. Approximately 300,000 tourists visit the island annually, and of these 182,000 arrive on cruise ships.

Gabled seventeenth century Dutch houses, painted in every pastel shade, give the visitor who arrives in Curaçao's capital city, Willemstad, a feeling that he is stepping into a tale by Hans Christian Anderson. This feeling of being a part of a happy fairy-tale persists as he comes to know the island.

Curaçao had a sleepy existence until 1914. The Dutch settled Curaçao in 1634. Here Peter Stuyvesant, who was later to be governor of New Amsterdam (New York), lost his leg. It was amputated following a wound received in battle, and legend says the leg is buried in the cemetery at Monte Verde on Curaçao. England occupied Curaçao briefly, but it was returned to The Netherlands in 1816.

Oil was discovered in Venezuela in 1914, and the following year the Royal Dutch Shell Company began to build one of the world's largest oil refineries on the island. Curaçao was off and running, and became one of the major commercial ports in the Caribbean.

In the 1950s the government launched a program to encourage tourism in order to give full employment to the citizenry. A luxurious hotel was built into the massive old seaside fort at Willemstad. The ramparts of the fort became a promenade for the guests. Tourists came, fell in love with the island, and many more resort hotels have been built with equal success. Curaçao is one of the most prosperous islands in the Caribbean today.

It is the largest island in the Netherlands Antilles, forty miles from Venezuela. Willemstad is the seat of government of the Dutch islands, active partners of Holland.

In Willemstad the Queen Emma Bridge, across St. Anna Bay, links the two parts of the city, Punda and Otrobanda. It swings open frequently during the day, causing pedestrians to scramble and automobiles to wait. A stroll across this pontoon bridge offers an excellent view of the colorful houses on the waterfront. The fairy-tale feeling persists in the fascinating "Floating Market," schooners loaded with fruits, vegetables and fabrics tied up in a canal beside the harbor.

The Mikve Israel Synagogue, close to the Floating Market, is the oldest synagogue in the Western Hemisphere, dating back to 1732. Beth Haim, the Jewish cemetery west of the city, was consecrated in 1659 and is possibly the oldest Caucasian burial place still in use in the Western Hemisphere. Among the first settlers were Jews who were fleeing the Spanish and Portuguese Inquisitions. They contributed greatly to the economic and cultural growth of the community.

Four statues recall others who contributed. Peter Stuyvesant stands in the garden of Stuyvesant College. Simon Bolivar, the South American liberator, looms large as a representative of the close relation between Curaçao and Venezuela. Pedro Luis Brión, a Curaçaon who harassed the English and Spanish in the nineteenth century as

Admiral of the Colombian fleet, dominates Brión Square. In Plaza Piar is the statue of Manuel Carlos Piar, a Curaçaon who became a Venezuelan general and conquered Guyana. Among the interesting historical buildings is the Old Dutch Reformed Church, rebuilt in 1796 within Fort Amsterdam. There is a fascinating museum in Willemstad with primitive artifacts and interesting historical material.

A ride through the countryside leads to excellent beaches on the leeward side of the island at Knip Bay, Piscadera Bay, Spanish Water, Santa Marta, Santa Cruz and Westpoint. A visit to the Hato Caves is fun. The caves have stalactites and stalagmites. They look like the kind of caves where primitive men might have painted on the walls. Here, however, *modern* man has done wall murals and the paintings are all lighted in a gaudy, jolly fashion.

The success of Curaçao's first luxury resort hotel has inspired the building of numerous other attractive hotels and guest rooms, plus lively gambling casinos. Visitors from North America, South America and Europe keep the rooms occupied. All sorts of water sports are available, and there are tennis courts, a golf course and gourmet meals at Curaçao's fine restaurants. The island's low import duties result in bargain shopping for luxury items from all over the world. Curaçao's bargains are famous among knowledgeable travellers. There is excellent jet service and many modern cruise ships make Willemstad a port-of-call.

Though Dutch is the official language of the island, Papiamento is the "lingua franca" of the people, as it is in Bonaire and Aruba. Curaçao not only has its own language, it also produces a unique liqueur, Curaçao, made from the peels of indigenous oranges.

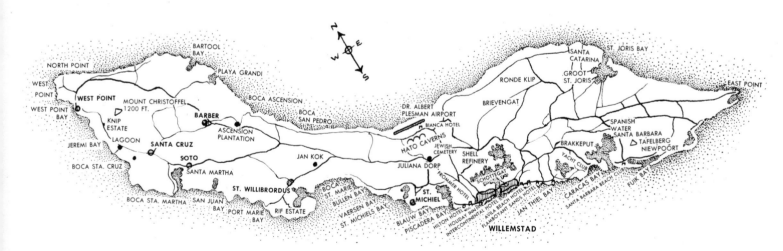

CURAÇAO

ARUBA

Magnificent beaches, a dry, healthy climate cooled by trade winds, and little rainfall make this an idyllic vacation island. The average temperature is 81° F. Aruba covers seventy-one square miles and has a population of 62,000. There are excellent resort hotels with gambling, good roads and freeport shopping. The capital, Oranjestad, has a fine, safe natural harbor. There are excellent airline connections to North and South America, Europe and other Caribbean islands. Approximately 196,000 visitors come annually, 60,000 on cruise ships. The languages spoken are Dutch, English, Spanish and Papiamento.

In huge bat-filled caves on the north coast of Aruba the first settlers left hieroglyphs painted in red dye on the cool cave walls. These first settlers were the Caribs. They gave trouble to the Arawaks who also lived on this island and left pottery as their relics.

It might almost be said that Aruba is that happy land that has no history. The island became a Dutch colony in 1634. Pirates attacked now and then, and a fort had to be built to keep them off. England seized and held the little island from 1805 to 1816, when it reverted to the Dutch. But the scene on Aruba for centuries was largely quiet and peaceful.

For a long time Aruba was a breeding ground for horses. In 1825 alluvial gold was found, but there was little of it. The cultivation of the aloe was promoted to alleviate the lack of industry and

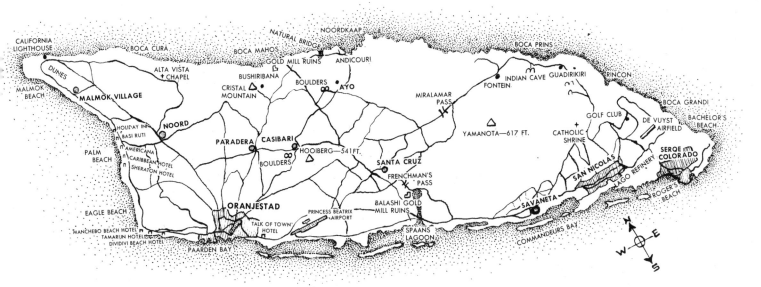

ARUBA

other feasible crops in the nineteenth century. Phosphate was mined at the southeast end of the island from 1874 until 1915, when mining ceased because the product couldn't compete on the international market.

Aruba is a serene and peaceful land today, but the economy changed dramatically for the better in the 1920s. Today it is one of the most prosperous and progressive islands in the Caribbean, with a high standard of living. Royal Dutch Shell built a small refinery on the island in 1924. Lago Oil and Transport Company, later purchased by Standard Oil of New Jersey, built one of the largest refineries in the world there in 1927. They refine Venezuelan oil. Lago has boosted the economy both by creating jobs and by being the island's largest taxpayer.

The economy received another big boost in 1958 when the government launched a program to attract tourists and investments. Because the beaches are beautiful, the climate is perfect and the people of Aruba are both gentle and competent, this program has been outstandingly successful.

Aruba is one of the Netherlands Antilles islands, which has a status similar to that of a commonwealth in relation to Holland. Each of the four island-territories has its own government with certain autonomous powers within the federation. Today Aruba has an excellent school system, no illiteracy. Most of the people speak three languages —Dutch, Papiamento and English. There is social security and a low rate of unemployment. Since it rarely rains in Aruba, water was once a problem. Now water is distilled from the sea by one of the world's largest distillation plants. Electricity is a by-product of the process.

The island is fifteen miles north of Venezuela. It is nineteen miles long and six miles wide. The most noticeable landmark is the 541 foot Hooiberg (Haystack Mountain), an extinct volcano that rises out of low land. Though it rarely rains, the cool, silken trade winds air-condition the land.

They not only blow dust and insects away, they blow so hard that the divi-divi trees all slant in the direction away from the prevailing wind. These distinctive trees are almost a trademark of Aruba.

As fast as new hotels are built on Aruba, their rooms are filled. Palm Beach, with its miles of white sand, is one of the most beautiful beaches in the Caribbean. There are numerous superb restaurants on the island. Casinos supply night-time excitement. Top entertainers come here for shows. Jet service is convenient.

For the athletic there is tennis, golf, bowling, basketball, volleyball, baseball and softball. Arubans are enthusiastic ping pong players, too. Reef fishing and deep-water fishing are excellent, and it is not unusual to hook a sailfish. A wreck of a vessel sunk by a German submarine is a hangout for all sorts of fish. Beautiful coral patches are close to the shore. These are perfect waters for skin-divers, and all facilities for water sports are available.

Oranjestad, the capital city, is a pastel Caribbean version of a little Dutch town, and it is pleasant to walk the clean and friendly streets. The deep harbor often has cruise ships at anchor. Free-port prices in excellent stores make shopping for everything from cameras to porcelain a favorite pursuit of visitors.

It is delightful to roam around the island, and the roads are good. The leeward shore on the southwest of the island is a sheltered coast with clear, tranquil green water and white sand beaches. The windward coast is exhilarating, with rough and rocky cliffs and pounding waves hurled out of blue depths. A favorite picnic spot is at the dramatic natural bridge carved from the rock by the waves at Andicouri on the windward shore. The Indian caves at Fontein on the north shore are fascinating. A climb up the Haystack Mountain is not strenuous and there's a fine view from the top.

Success has not spoiled Aruba. This island is still serene, a land of happy people and soothing beauty.

JAMAICA

This independent state is a member of the British Commonwealth and the United Nations and its agencies, an affiliate of the World Bank, and a member of the Organization of American States and the Caribbean Free Trade Association. This large island has magnificent scenery, beautiful mountains and beaches, luxurious resorts, fine roads, excellent hotel accommodations, several outstanding golf courses, horse racing, polo, river rafting, sailing, tennis, fishing, water skiing, night clubs and fascinating folklore shows. The capital is Kingston. It covers 4,412 square miles, has a population of 2,000,000. Excellent airline connections are available to North and South America, Europe and other Caribbean islands. English is the language. Annually 420,000 visitors come to Jamaica, about 172,000 on cruise ships.

Jamaica, with 4,400 square miles of land, is not only one of the larger islands of the world, it is also one of the most varied in its charms. It has been described as a continent in miniature. White sand shores give place to lush green vegetation, which changes as the observer goes from the lowlands to the alpine heights. Third largest of the Caribbean islands, it is 144 miles long, fifty miles wide.

Columbus came ashore on Jamaica in 1494 on his second adventure in the New World. He named the island Santiago and claimed it for Spain. He made his landing at a beautiful bay on the north coast which he called Gloria.

The Spanish began to settle the island in 1509, when Juan de Esquivel arrived as the first Spanish governor. They established a colony that raised cattle, pigs, sheep, oranges, bananas and other crops. They enslaved the Arawaks, who promptly died, and then brought in the first slaves from Africa about 1517. Initially the principal city was Sevilla Nueva (New Seville), on the north coast. Later the Spaniards moved their main settlement to the southern coast where they built a new headquarters, Santiago de la Vega (St. James of the Plain). Today that settlement, which lies west of Kingston, is known as Spanish Town.

The Spaniards made little effort to develop Jamaica. English privateers and pirates of all nations raided the island. In 1655 an English force on an expedition ordered by the Lord Protector of England, Oliver Cromwell, took Kingston Harbour and the Spanish surrendered. Though the Spanish continued a long guerrilla war against the British from the mountains, Jamaica became a British colony. Runaway Bay on the north coast was the departure point of the last resisting Spaniard, Don Arnaldo de Ysassi, who fled in 1660.

African slaves fought beside the Spanish during those years, and it was then that the Maroon colony of freed Africans was established in the mountains. English settlers and a small colony of Jews immigrated to the island during the latter years of the seventeenth century, and the Maroons continued to live on in the mountains in isolated freedom. They regularly raided the English colonies on the plains. After years of proving that the English colonists could not conquer them and their guerrilla bands, the Maroons in 1739 signed a treaty with the British which gave them tax-free land and self-rule. The treaty is still in force today, and the Maroons live peaceably and industriously in their mountain homes.

As sugar cane grew in importance, Jamaica grew in wealth. Planters with money to build sugar mills arrived, and imported African slaves to do the work. There were 10,000 white people and 130,000 slaves on the island in 1750. Britain established a legislative system and built forts to protect what was becoming a rich prize.

Pirates and buccaneers, who were condoned by the authorities, made Port Royal their headquarters, and it became "the wealthiest and wickedest city on the face of the earth." Legends of raids still abound. Port Royal was shaken by an earthquake in 1692 and slid into the sea.

The last half of the eighteenth century was the era of the great sugar-producing estates in Jamaica. There were numerous slave revolutions, until the slave trade was abolished in 1838 and modern Jamaica was born. In fact that year many ex-slaves left the estates and became farmers in their own hill villages. East Indians were brought in to till the fields as indentured laborers between 1845 and 1917. Chinese also immigrated and became shopkeepers, and the Lebanese who arrived at the end of the nineteenth century became successful merchants.

Kingston was built to replace Port Royal. It is the capital of Jamaica and the largest English-speaking city in the Caribbean today. Roads and railroads were built and extended, schools and hospitals were established. The principal exports continued to be sugar, rum, coffee, tobacco, cocoa and bananas. By 1955, when Jamaica celebrated three hundred years as a British colony, the island had full internal constitutional self-government. Jamaica achieved full independence as a member of the British Commonwealth in 1962, and is now a free and sovereign land.

Sunshine and calypso, rafting down a river, sophisticated resorts, theater, sports, dancing, fishing and native cabaret shows—the entertainment offered to vacationers in Jamaica is delightful and varied. The mountainous island has five distinctly different resort areas, all linked by good roads.

Kingston on the southern coast is the capital city and the heart of the island's life. Among the many delightful spots to visit around Kingston are the world-famous Royal Botanical Gardens, the historical remains in Port Royal and Spanish Town, the museum and gallery at the Institute of Jamaica, and the attractive University of the West Indies at the foothills of the Blue Mountains.

Port Antonio, beside the sea on the northeast coast, is a mecca for fishermen and offers rafting on the beautiful Rio Grande. Here the Jamaica International Fishing Tournament is held each autumn. The Blue Lagoon is a center of recreation.

Ocho Rios, one of the oldest areas of the island, lies on the north coast, and has interesting remains of the early days of Spanish colonization. Here the Spaniards first landed at Discovery Bay, and left from Runaway Bay. Nearby are two spectacular waterfalls, at Fern Gully and Dunn's River.

Montego Bay on the northwest shore is the sophisticated and famed winter resort area. The luxurious hotels with their entertainment, splendid white sand beaches at Doctor's Cave, and clear green waters draw many visitors.

Mandeville lies 2,000 feet above sea level in the cool and lofty central hills of the island, and is a peaceful and picturesque resort. Known as Jamaica's "English village," its stimulating climate and leisurely pace attract vacationers.

Visitors are also lured to Jamaica by all sorts of water sports, championship golf courses and horse-racing at Caymanas Park in Kingston. Yachtsmen find excellent facilities. Tourism is one of the island's major industries, and Jamaica has plenty of natural and man-made attractions.

Fertile soils and fine climate produce diverse crops. Cattle, sugar cane and bananas continue to be the principal produce. Bauxite mining is one of the newest and most important of Jamaica's industries.

The people of Jamaica are predominantly of African descent, with a liberal admixture of European ancestors and some Chinese and East Indian blood. Their language is English—a seventeenth century English sprinkled with African words. Their music is the lilting calypso, their culture and customs a product of many lands and many people. The vigorous Jamaicans today are showing the world how to achieve a peaceful and harmonious nation from a multi-racial heritage. It is a land not only rich in beauty, climate and legend— it also has a viable and progressive economy, oriented toward a developing future.

CAYMAN ISLANDS

The three Cayman Islands are a British colony. Largest is Grand Cayman, with George Town as its capital. These are flat islands with beautiful beaches and good hotels, a paradise for fishermen and divers. There are airports on Grand Cayman and Cayman Brac, and a private airstrip on Little Cayman. They contain ninety-nine square miles, with a population of 12,000. The average temperature is 78° F. A green turtle hatchery is operated by Mariculture, Ltd. on Grand Cayman. The language is English. Approximately 84,000 tourists visit annually, 26,000 arriving on cruise ships.

The three small Cayman Islands lie south of Cuba in the heart of the Caribbean. Grand Cayman is about two hundred miles northwest of Jamaica. It is twenty-three miles long by eight miles wide at its widest. Cayman Brac, fifty-eight miles to the northeast of Grand Cayman, is twelve miles long and one mile wide. "Brac" is an old English word that means cliff, and the island is really a cliff rising from the sea, with a fertile plateau on top. Little Cayman, ten by two miles, is five miles north of Brac. All are linked by boat and by air. They are all British colonies originally settled by seamen and the sea is still the principal means of livelihood.

Columbus sailed past the islands on his fourth voyage and named them "Tortugas," turtle islands, because the Spaniards sighted crowds of turtles about the shores. Another explorer came along and was apparently impressed by the alligators he saw, for he changed the name to Cayman. ("Caiman" is the Spanish word for alligator.) There are no alligators living there now, but huge sea turtles still lay eggs on the beaches. Sea turtles were easily portable meat for sailing vessels, and it was only for these turtles that sailing ships came to the islands for decades. There were no Spanish settlers there when the British took possession in 1670, though before and after numerous notorious pirates came to the turtle-rich islands.

When ten British ships were wrecked offshore of East End in a storm in 1788, Caymanians risked their lives in small row-boats to rescue those aboard. Henceforth the islanders were exempted by King George III from paying taxes for all time. They are today, by choice, Crown Colonies of Great Britain and pay no income, property or inheritance taxes. Caymanians are skilled sailors and engineers, and many island families are supported by money seamen send home.

There are numerous hotels especially on a beautiful beach, Seven Mile Beach, near George Town on the west coast. Other delightful beaches are at Frank Sound and Collier's Point, and also along a stretch of the north shore. The principal towns of Grand Cayman are George Town, the capital, West Bay, Bodden Town, East End and Northside. All lie beside the sea. On Cayman Brac the settlements are Stake Bay, Creek, Spot Bay and West End. Blossom Village is Little Cayman's only settlement.

The waters around the infertile volcanic islands are rich in fish and lobsters, the clawless tropical variety known as crawfish. North Sound, off the western end of Grand Cayman, is great for fishing and sailing. The reefs that surround the islands are a delight to scuba divers and undersea explorers, and relics of many sunken ships can be spotted in crystal-clear waters on the once pirate-haunted reefs.

The Caymanians by some blessed alchemy, have become among the friendliest people of the world. Approximately 54% are of mixed racial origin, 20% of European, 26% of African descent. There is no racial friction in the Caymans.

And then, just a few years ago they became one of the great tax havens of the world. The Cayman Islands passed laws, that are very good to money invested there, including number accounts with high interest payments. Some of the very rich of the Western World put their money in Caymanian banks today rather than in Swiss banks. There are 193 banks in George Town, capital of the Cayman Islands.

These islands have become especially appealing to people from North America — people that range from the rich to divers. Caymanians speak English with a Welsh lilt that is touching to the heart. International affairs of the islands are handled by Great Britain, through the Governor. The Cayman laws regarding taxation couldn't be better. Investors, courted by these laws, have built splendid accommodations for visitors — luxurious hotels and apartments. (There are modest quarters, too.) Jets fly in daily. Everybody gets happier all the time in the Cayman Islands.

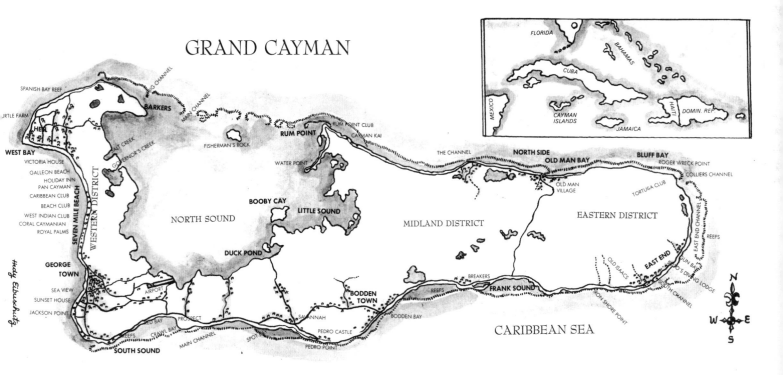

GRAND CAYMAN

CUBA

Largest of the Caribbean islands, Cuba has beautiful scenery, colorful cities and good beaches. It contains 44,218 square miles, 8,100,000 people. The government is a democratic socialist republic, and Havana is the capital. The most important products are agricultural: sugar, coffee, tobacco and livestock. There is good fishing around the island. There are regular airline connections to Europe, Central and South America.

La Republica de Cuba includes not only the island of Cuba but also the Isle of Pines, a smaller island just south of the western end of Cuba. There are also numerous small cays and islands. The long, narrow island stretches 760 miles from east to west and is twenty-five to 125 miles in width. It lies ninety miles south of the Florida Keys.

This is a green and flowering land with sheltered bays and cliffs along the north coast, where the mountains drop sharply into the sea. The southern coast is low and swampy. There are splendid stretches of white sand beaches. The fertile fields of the western and central section produce sugar cane and tobacco, and cattle ranching is found on less fertile land in the east central part, especially in the province of Camaguey. Pico de Turquino, the highest peak, rises 6,562 feet in the rugged Oriente province. Short rivers run to the sea, and the 150-mile Cauto River is the longest river. The Isle of Pines is hilly, well-wooded.

The climate of Cuba is practically perfect, with summers air-conditioned by the cooling trade winds, and winters that are almost always frost-free. The average annual temperature is 76°F. The south coast is cooler than the north coast and the interior of the island is cooler than the coast. The rainy season begins toward the end of May and extends through October. Rainfall is heavier in the west and in the interior of the island, and heavier on the north coast than the south.

Columbus sighted the island on October 27, 1492, on his first voyage, and he landed on the north coast. He thought he had found Japan or China, though he named the land Juana, for the King of Spain. Later the name was changed to Santiago, and then to Ave Maria, until finally the original Indian name was restored.

The original Indian inhabitants were conquered in 1511 by Diego Velásquez, who founded Baracoa, Santiago and Havana, the capital, which was established on the north coast beside a good harbor in 1519. Rumors of gold drew many early settlers. The first slaves were brought from Africa in 1523, and by 1544 practically all the Indians had been killed by the Spaniards. Havana became a major base for Spanish expeditions exploring Mexico, Peru and Florida. For more than a century the plate fleet laden with gold rendezvoused in Havana harbor on its way back home to Spain.

Except for a brief period when the British occupied Havana in 1762 and 1763 the island remained Spanish until it achieved its independence. The British returned Cuba to Spain in 1763 and were given Florida in exchange. Many Spaniards moved to Cuba when Jamaica became English and Santo Domingo was ceded to France. Chinese coolies were imported until 1871.

Under a liberal Spanish constitutional government and with Spanish Governors who had a light hand on the reins, Cuba thrived in the late

GULF OF MEXICO

HAVANA

ATLANTIC OCEAN

N

S

PINAR DEL RIO

PINAR DEL RIO

HAVANA

MANTUA

MATANZAS

GULF OF BATABANO

LAS VILLAS

CAMAGÜEY

CIENFUEGOS

CAMAGÜEY

ISLA DE PINOS

CARIBBEAN SEA

ORIENTE

CUBA

SIERRA MAESTRA

SANTIAGO DE CUBA

eighteenth and early nineteenth centuries. Then came a series of heavy-handed military tyrants from Spain and discontent flared into civil revolution in 1868. Reforms followed. Slavery was abolished in 1886 and in 1893 blacks and whites were given equal civil status. José Marti led the final fight for independence, which began in 1895 and ended on December 10, 1898, after the U.S. entered the war.

Politically the Negro has been the white man's equal throughout the twentieth century. Spanish slave laws were always comparatively generous and there is almost no color caste on the island. When Columbus first saw Cuba the land was heavily and beautifully wooded and had many valuable hardwoods. Much of the land has been cleared for farming. The native flora includes more than

thirty species of native palms and many cedar trees that of old were used to manufacture cigar boxes. Cuba also has manganese, iron, chrome, copper, oil and cobalt.

The majority of workers are engaged in agriculture, fishing and mining, though industry is increasing. The principal crops are sugar, tobacco, coffee and livestock—cattle, pigs and poultry. Cocoa, pineapples, vegetables and rice are also important crops. Tractors have been imported in recent years and the use of fertilizers has increased. Chief exports of Cuba today are sugar, tobacco, coffee, rum and molasses. The surrounding waters are rich in fish, which constitute an important part of the Cuban diet, and there is a large fishing fleet.

Cuba has a well-developed road system with a central highway running the length of the island from Pinár del Rio through Havana to Santiago. There are numerous fine natural landlocked harbors, in addition to Havana harbor. Radio, television, telephones, telegrams and the postal service are controlled by the Ministry of Communications.

Education is free and compulsory and the rate of illiteracy has been sharply reduced in the last decade. There are three universities, one in Havana, one in Santa Clara and one in Santiago de Cuba. The predominating religion is Roman Catholic, though Cuba's constitution guarantees complete religious freedom. Rum is the national drink. Baseball has become the nation's favorite sport. Havana, a beautiful city, is distinguished by the fine modern Palace of Fine Arts, lovely old Cathedral Square, and numerous other historically interesting buildings and forts.

The Isle of Pines, thirty-five miles off the southern coast of Cuba, is sometimes called "Treasure Island." It became a Cuban possession in 1925. It is a scenic vacation mecca with rolling hills, fine forests and lovely gardens. Nueva Gerona is the capital. It has excellent hunting and fishing.

HAITI

Most exotic country in the Caribbean Is the independent republic of Haiti on the western end of the island of Hispaniola. It covers 10,700 square miles and has a population 6,000,000 people. Beautiful mountains rise up to 9,000 feet in height. The capital is Port-au-Prince. There are fascinating historical monuments such as the Citadel and the Palace of Sans Souci, and old towns. The people, culture, religion and folklore are unique and absorbing. There are excellent hotel facilities, nightclubs and gambling casinos. Good airline connections are offered to North and South America, Europe and the Caribbean islands. Recreations include golf, tennis, hunting, fishing, art exhibits and cock fights. French and English are the languages. About 292,000 visitors come each year, and of these 195,000 arrive on cruise ships.

Exciting, vivid in its beauty, Haiti, the first black republic in the Caribbean, is a land like nowhere else on earth. It is a unique mixture of African and French culture, full of exotic contrasts. Here visitors can enjoy cock-fighting, hunting, gambling, art collecting, nightclubbing, golfing, fishing, undersea exploring and mountain-climbing in surroundings graced with a natural grandeur.

Haiti takes its name from the Arawak word "Hayti," which means The Mountain Country. It occupies the western one-third of the island of Hispaniola with the Dominican Republic on the eastern two-thirds of the island. The Haitians are descended from slaves who came from the Congo, the Gold Coast, Sudan and Senegal, and their blood is laced with that of French plantation owners. The Spaniards came to Hispaniola first, but it had no gold, and they did not do much in the way of settlement in the western part of the island. In the seventeenth century France settled what they called St. Domingue and imported so many slaves that the white Frenchmen were soon outnumbered by more than ten to one.

136

Haiti

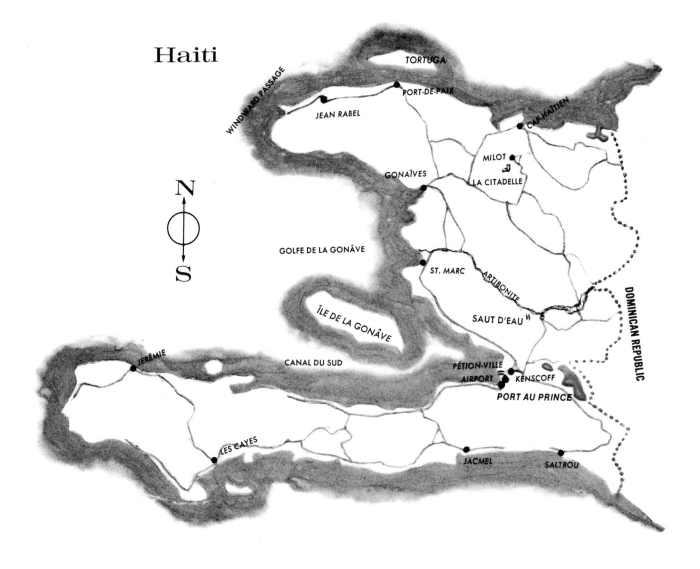

The great uprising in Haiti came in the midst of the French Revolution. Blacks rose up against mulattoes and their white masters. Toussaint L'Ouverture, Jean Jacques Dessalines and King Henri Christophe were the great black leaders in Haiti's war of independence. Since then the politi-cal history of the country has been stormy, but Haiti has been free of foreign rulers.

Hispaniola is the most mountainous island of the Caribbean, and the peaks of Haiti reach to 9,000 feet. The steep land has a network of trails, paths and rough roads leading through rugged beauty. Parts of the country are still largely unexplored.

Port-au-Prince is the capital of Haiti. It combines narrow streets in its old sections with broad boulevards in the newer parts of town. Peasants driving donkeys come in to sell fruits and politicos are driven about in limousines. Massive colonial buildings shelter shops that sell a wide array of imported luxuries to tourists, but the most exciting objects for sale are the primitive paintings and the polished wood carvings. They speak the universal tongue of art with an accent that is uniquely Haitian. Among the interesting places to visit in Port-au-Prince is the National Museum, which has many historical exhibits. They include the anchor of Columbus' flagship, the Santa Maria, which sank off Hispaniola on the first voyage.

In the Episcopal Cathedral of the Holy Trinity are fine murals, the most important single series of paintings in the primitive Haitian style. The Iron Market is one of the great flea markets of the world, with irresistible opportunities for the impulsive shopper. Attractive grace notes in the street scenes of Port-au-Prince are the sidewalk cafés, French in inspiration, Caribbean in flavor. The palace of the President is modelled after the Petit Palace in Paris.

Cap-Haïtien, which is called Le Cap, is the second largest city in the country. King Henri Christophe had the royal palace of Sans Souci built for himself here as a Versailles of the New World. The palace, now in ruins, had spacious galleries, panelled rooms, mirrored walls, splendid paintings and 365 doors. It also had a non-electric air-conditioning system.

The most exciting man-made structure in Haiti is the breathtaking fortress La Citadelle, built by Henri Christophe. It is an impregnable fortress high in the mountains near Cap Haitien, reached only by a rough trail. There is nothing like it in the Caribbean. It is built on the scale of ancient Egyptian and Roman monuments to kings and gods. Christophe built it to house ten thousand troops. The walls are twelve feet thick at the base, 140 feet high. The stones are huge. Twenty thousand ex-slaves died in its building. It is a monument to mighty architectural engineering, and to the mighty dreams that haunt the ruin. If there were nothing else, a visit to La Citadelle is worth a trip to Haiti.

But there is so much else. There are the ruins of Pauline Bonaparte's castle at Cap Haïtien. There is voodoo. Many of the voodoo rites about Port-au-Prince are staged for tourists, but true voodoo lives in Haiti. It is an African religion in which themes of the Catholic church are interwoven. It is primitive, symbolic, with drums, dancing, wild gyrations, walking through fire, sacrifice of animals. There are, however, no crucifixions. Cock-fights, too, are a bloody aspect of Haitian recreation. They draw gamblers who glory in a contest between two birds that will fight until the death rattle.

A delightful expedition may be made by glass bottom boat to the magnificent coral reef, Sand Cay, five miles from shore in the Baie de Port-au-Prince. It is one of the most magnificent coral reefs in the islands. The wonderful canyons built by the corals are full of beautiful sea creatures, moving with liquid grace in a panorama of exotic beauty.

The International Casino in Port-au-Prince offers gaming in the continental manner. The island has excellent resort hotels that offer fine food, dancing and sophisticated entertainment. The rewards for those who visit and explore this vivid country are rich memories of an exciting land.

DOMINICAN REPUBLIC

The land that Columbus loved best is a large rich country covering 19,129 square miles of the eastern part of the island of Hispaniola. The population is 4,850,000, the capital, Santo Domingo, where Columbus is buried. High mountains in the north rise up to 10,490 feet. The flat lands of the south are fertile and highly developed agriculturally, with good roads. This land has the oldest colonial historical monuments in the Western Hemisphere and is also rich in Indian artifacts. There are excellent hotel accommodations, nightclubs, gambling casinos, golf, polo, tennis, sailing and fishing. Airlines connect with North and South and Central America, Europe and other Caribbean islands. The languages are Spanish and English. Approximately 250,000 tourists visit annually. — It is a democratic republic of 26 provinces, governed by a president, Senate and Chamber of Deputies, freely elected every four years.

The Dominican Republic, on the eastern two-thirds of the island called Hispaniola, is the land that Columbus loved best, and anybody can see why. High, majestic mountains rise behind the principal city, Santo Domingo. The valleys and the plains are fertile, and support sugar cane, bananas and cattle, horse ranches and mahogany forests. The beaches are beautiful, the clear waters filled with fish and lobster. The flavor of life is Spanish.

Columbus sighted the island on his first voyage in 1492. The Admiral's brother, Bartolomé, settled the capital, Santo Domingo, in 1496. It is the oldest city in the New World. Here Columbus, who died in Spain, was re-buried. His bones lie in the great Cathedral of Santa Maria la Menor in a splendid marble sepulcher. His son, Diego, built his fortress home here. It is called the Alcázar and is a colonial architectural gem, carefully restored and rebuilt. While it was being built Diego Columbus lived in the House of Cord. That house, which dates back to 1502, is the oldest house in the Western World.

Santo Domingo was the hub of Spain's colonial empire in the West Indies. Cortés, Ponce de León, Pizarro and Balboa used it as a base for their explorations. But there was no gold on the island, and the gold that the Spaniards found in Mexico and Peru distracted their attention from this colony. Sir Francis Drake raided and plundered Santo Domingo. French buccaneers took over the western one-third of the island, which later became Haiti. In 1822 the Haitians conquered what is now the Dominican Republic and occupied it until 1844. In a revolution in that year the Dominican Republic was born and since then it has been practically an independent nation. Political disorder followed for more than a century. Trujillo ruled as a dictator for three decades, until he was assassinated in 1961.

In recent years the politics and the economy of the country have become stable. Santo Domingo, La Romana, Boca Chica on the south coast, Puerto Plata on the north coast, Jarabacoa, La Vega, Santiago, Constanza in the mountains have good hotels and resorts. Modern highways take visitors to the countryside and to popular resorts. Santo Domingo is an elegant capital, with wide and beautiful boulevards, fine homes, lovely parks, a huge outdoor theater and casinos.

In addition to the tomb of Columbus, the magnificent Cathedral Santa Maria la Menor has some splendid treasures of colonial Spain, including a fortune in jewels, paintings by Murillo and silver by Cellini. It is one of the finest relics of colonial times in the Caribbean, and is lovingly preserved. Numerous other colonial churches are equally cherished. Pre-

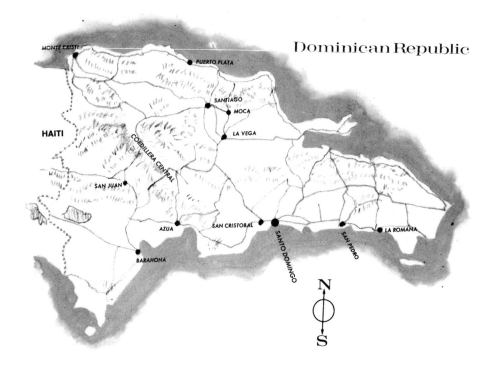

Dominican Republic

Colombian Indian artifacts and carvings are displayed in the National Museum. The museum itself was once the stables and servants' quarters of Diego Columbus. One of the interesting reminders of the past is the stump of a silk cotton tree, the Columbus Ceiba. Here, it is claimed, Columbus tied his ship when he dropped anchor in the Ozama River. Parks and botanical gardens lure nature-loving natives and visitors, and there are caves with pre-historic petroglyphs.

The Plaza de la Cultura, former site of the Trujillo mansion, is now a beautiful, expansive park which houses the following cultural centers: The Gallery of Modern Art, a collection of national and international paintings, sculpture and period furniture with emphasis on native artists. — The Museum of Natural History and Science. — The National Library, a center of education in the West Indies. — The National Theatre, a showplace for opera, concerts, classical ballet and folkloric dance.

Boca Chica, 5 miles east of Santo Domingo, is the principal beach resort in the capital area. Puerto Plata, Port of Silver, 130 miles northwest of Santo Domingo is the main city on the north shore, port for many cruise ships. Bordered by the Cordillera mountain range, the city has a cable car ride to Isabel de Torres peak (2,565 ft.) and also beautiful beaches.

Exploration of the mountains is a great adventure, for they are filled with rushing rivers, waterfalls, splendid woodlands. Jarabacoa and Constanza are two of the attractive mountain towns with good accommodations for travellers.

ACKNOWLEDGMENTS

For the preparation of this book I had the valuable cooperation of Jane Wood Reno, who checked and edited the manuscript; I had the assistance of my son Michael Hannau, of Paul Hogan, Karl Mayer and Wim ter Hart. Some material was used from my previous books on the Caribbean, which were prepared with the assistance of others. My sincere appreciation goes to all who contributed to this volume.

Hans W. Hannau

INDEX

THE PICTURES